# RECOLLECTION, TESTIMONY, and LYING

## in Early Childhood

The LAW AND PUBLIC POLICY: PSYCHOLOGY AND THE SOCIAL SCIENCES series includes books in three domains:

*Legal Studies*—writings by legal scholars about issues of relevance to psychology and the other social sciences, or that employ social science information to advance the legal analysis;

*Social Science Studies*—writings by scientists from psychology and the other social sciences about issues of relevance to law and public policy; and

*Forensic Studies*—writings by psychologists and other mental health scientists and professionals about issues relevant to forensic mental health science and practice.

The series is guided by its editor, Bruce D. Sales, PhD, JD, University of Arizona; and coeditors, Stephen J. Ceci, PhD, Cornell University; Norman J. Finkel, PhD, Georgetown University; and Bruce J. Winick, JD, University of Miami.

• • •

# RECOLLECTION, TESTIMONY, and LYING

## in Early Childhood

CLARA STERN
WILLIAM STERN

JAMES T. LAMIELL, Translator

AMERICAN PSYCHOLOGICAL ASSOCIATION
Washington, DC

Published by
American Psychological Association
750 First Street, NE
Washington, DC 20002

Copies may be ordered from
APA Order Department
P.O. Box 92984
Washington, DC 20090-2984

In the U.K. and Europe, copies may be ordered from
American Psychological Association
3 Henrietta Street
Covent Garden, London
WC2E 8LU England

Typeset in Goudy by EPS Group Inc., Easton, MD
Printer: Braun-Brumfield, Inc., Ann Arbor, MI
Cover Designer: DRI Consulting, Chevy Chase, MD
Editor/Project Manager: Debbie K. Hardin, Reston, VA

**Library of Congress Cataloging-in-Publication Data**
Stern, Clara.
    [Erinnerung, Aussage und Lüge in der ersten Kindheit. English]
    Recollection, testimony, and lying in early childhood / by William
& Clara Stern : translated by James T. Lamiell.
        p.   cm.
    Clara Stern's name appears first on original German language
edition.
    Includes bibliographical references (p.    ) and index.
    ISBN 1-55798-574-X
    1. Memory in children.   2. Recollection (Psychology)
3. Truthfulness and falsehood in children.   4. Child witnesses.
I. Stern, William, 1871–1938.   II. Title.
BF723.M4S7413   1999
155.4'1312—dc21                                        98-13102
                                                           CIP

**British Library Cataloguing-in-Publication Data**
A CIP record is available from the British Library.

*Printed in the United States of America*
*First Edition*

To Leslie, whose ways with children I so admire.

# CONTENTS

# ABOUT THE AUTHORS

**Clara Joseephy** was born into a well-to-do Berlin family on March 2, 1878. As a young woman, she was discouraged from pursuing university studies, and so never earned an advanced degree. Nevertheless, her sharp mind and keen observational skills enabled her to make indispensable contributions to the collaborative research effort that would yield (among other works) the present volume. After her marriage to William Stern in 1899, Clara Stern became the person most responsible for keeping the diaries that, over a period of 18 years, would archive countless, multifaceted observations relevant to the psychological development of the couple's three children, Hilde, Günther, and Eva. The first of two monographs coauthored by the Sterns and based largely on earlier portions of the diary material was *Die Kindersprache* (*Children's Speech*), published in 1907. The second of the two monographs was the present work, which appeared in 1909 under the title *Erinnerung, Aussage, und Lüge in der ersten Kindheit*. William Stern would later describe Clara's signal contributions to these works as those of a woman possessed of "an intuitive, motherly understanding of what makes children tick, combined with an unerring observational objectivity and a prudent caution in the interpretation of what had been observed. Added to this was a lively writing style and an indefatigable diligence in the completion of a task once begun." With her husband, Clara Stern fled Germany shortly after Hitler's rise to power in 1933, and resided in Durham, North Carolina, until William's death in 1938. Subsequently, she resided in New York. After becoming a U.S. citizen, she earned a living during World War II assisting the American effort to censor German-language letters. Clara Stern died in New York on December 8, 1945.

**Louis William Stern** was born in Berlin to Jewish parents of modest means on April 29, 1871. William (as he would come to be known) was educated at the Friedrich-Wilhelms-University in Berlin, concentrating his studies in philology, philosophy, and psychology. In 1897, Stern followed his Berlin professor Hermann Ebbinghaus to the University of Breslau (now Wroclaw, Poland), and it was there where Stern collaborated with wife Clara on the several works, including the present one, which would be based on the aforementioned diaries. After moving with the entire family to Hamburg in 1916, William Stern was a major figure in the establishment of the university there 3 years later, and he served that institution for the next 14 years as professor of psychology and philosophy. It was during the Hamburg years that Stern completed his three-volume magnum opus, a work he titled *Person and Thing: The System of Critical Personalism*. Through these three volumes, consisting of *Philosophical Foundations* (1906), *The Human Personality* (1918), and *Philosophy of Values* (1924), Stern set forth a comprehensive conception of human persons and their interrelationships within communities that would be, in his own words, "as far removed from a one-sided individualism recognizing only the rights and happiness of the single individual, as from a socialism in which individuality and personal freedom are choked by the pressures of supra-personal demands."

Fleeing Germany in 1934, the Sterns went first to Holland, where William completed his last major work, *General Psychology From a Personalistic Standpoint*. He then accepted an offer to join the psychology faculty at Duke University. William Stern died in Durham, North Carolina, on March 27, 1938.

# FOREWORD

## THE LEGACY OF CLARA AND WILLIAM STERN: REDISCOVERING THE ORIGINS OF CONTEMPORARY VIEWS ON THE CHILD WITNESS

STEPHEN J. CECI AND MAGGIE BRUCK

In 1909, Clara and William Stern first published *Recollection, Testimony, and Lying in Early Childhood*, the second of their "Monographs on the Psychological Development of the Child." At this time, the field of developmental psychology was still in its metaphorical infancy. Little was known about children's emergent cognitive and social development, James Baldwin's and G. Stanley Hall's ideas were still obscure, and Jean Piaget was not yet a force. The Sterns had little in the way of a developmental theory to guide them as they embarked on what would later come to be seen as a monumental chronicling of the development of their three children.

Lamiell deserves the admiration and gratitude of all contemporary monolingual Anglophones for the skill and care he took in making this work available to us for the first time in its entirety. Readers will discover a rich vein of thinking in this monograph that will spawn new hypotheses.

The Sterns' thinking proved to be so far ahead of its time that an argument can be made that much of the research carried out in the half century that followed was derivative of their ideas. Indeed, much of what they wrote in this monograph could, with very minor stylistic changes, be inserted into any modern text on memory development without the reader detecting the slightest hint of its antiquity. So prescient was the Sterns' scholarship that it adumbrated most of the current debate about whether children are more suggestible than adults, and if so, whether the nature of their suggestibility is such that they ought to be precluded from testifying in court. No matter which current issue in cognitive development you choose, it is covered in Lamiell's masterful translation of this monograph. It is a cornucopia of ideas that remain in the forefront of developmental psychology.

The Sterns understood the role of individual differences in suggestibility, the concepts of *reminiscence* and *reactivation* and the idea that suggestibility can emanate from both cognitive (retrieval-time blending, source confusions, and memory overwrite) as well as social sources (motivations and conscious lies). They provide a cogent distinction between lying and false beliefs that is fully current, pointing out both the volitional and declarative aspects of children's denials. The Sterns were far ahead of their time in noting the importance of studying social class and child-rearing effects on testimony, topics of great current interest.

To one working in this field today, the extent to which the Sterns' thinking foreshadowed current debates is eerie. Have we been reinventing the wheel, transferring old wine into new bottles? Such a conclusion is probably overly harsh, ignoring the many methodological advances that have been made that allow for tests of ideas the Sterns were unable to test themselves. Nevertheless, one emerges from reading this century-old monograph with a tremendous respect for these fine scholars. Their reasoning was as complex as that which can be found in the best developmental journals today.

On the question of individual differences in suggestibility: "The collection of mistaken recollections we have registered for Hilde [the eldest of the three children they studied] is relatively small . . . attributable in part to the psychological makeup of the child" (p. 27) In this instance we see an early recognition of what is now the busiest area of suggestibility research—namely, the degree to which individual differences interact with situational factors to determine a child's level of suggestibility. Throughout the work, there is ample documentation of individual differences—in resisting leading questions, in lying, and in spatial and color perception.

The Sterns' concept of *reminiscence* is another of their thoroughly modern foreshadowings. Reminiscence refers to the recollection of new information with each new recall attempt, information that was not recalled on a previous recall attempt. The Sterns were aware of reminiscence and the role that it played in consolidating memory. Consider: "Later recollections are not simply calling to mind her earlier recall-based accounts. This is especially apparent from the fact that in the later instances of thinking back, elements appear that had not been mentioned in the earlier instances" (p. 24). Closely related to this is their early detection of what is known presently as *reactivation*, the tendency for a test trial to bolster later recollections. They provide the earliest evidence of this effect of which we are aware. Indeed, this remains a fruitful area of exploration among developmentalists (e.g., Rovee-Collier, 1993).

On the topic of recall accuracy, the Sterns assert what has become the mantra of developmentalists in the past decade—namely, that the free recall of very young children is sparse, but the little they do recall tends to be highly accurate. Consider: "Spontaneous testimony is not as susceptible to errors as is testimony in response to questioning" (p. 28) Yet the Sterns also noted the downside of free recall: "Freely given reports lack specificity with respect to time, a feature that is as significant for the value of the testimony as it is dangerous for the testimony's accuracy" (p. 28). In 1993, when we reviewed the literature in this area, we came to the same conclusion, based on modern research (Ceci & Bruck, 1993). The Sterns knew it nearly a century earlier.

The role of expectancies on report accuracy is another prescient idea seen in the Sterns' description of the time Hilde was shown a picture of two eagles attacking a sea gull against a stormy sky. At the time, Hilde was 46 months old. The Sterns were unsuccessful in inducing Hilde to succumb to the suggestion that the eagles had been on the ground as opposed to being airborne when they attacked the seagull. But Hilde nevertheless reported that the sky in the picture was blue and the eagles were brown, characteristics that normally apply but were not part of the picture she had been shown. Hilde made a similar mistake when, at the age of 72 months, she claimed that a bust of Goethe was sitting on a piano in a particular room. In reality, it was located in a different room of the Sterns' new home, although the position Hilde had indicated did indeed correspond to the position the bust had occupied 10 months previously, in the Sterns' former residence. All of this is familiar terrain to today's experimentalists who do similar studies.

The Sterns' view of the important role that expectations play in recollection was not limited to laboratory-type observations that entail showing children pictures, but extended to daily perceptions and experiences of the young child. The Sterns describe an instance when daughter Hilde was 46 months old and walking one day with her mother in the park. She had on previous occasions seen the swans that live in the park, but on the particular day in question, the swans were not to be seen as the pond was frozen over. The relevant entry from the Sterns' diaries read as follows: "As we walked along, I asked Hilde 'What did we see?' She answered promptly, 'We have seen swans.' I [Clara Stern]: 'Did we really see swans?' Hilde: 'No, they were inside the huts.' . . . This shows that the content of something in which one's interest has been strongly stimulated can seem to have been actually experienced even in the absence of perception" (p. 29).

The Sterns noted a pattern that some today might find objectionable. They argued that children often give answers to questions about events that they did not initially pay attention to. For instance, when Hilde was asked about the colors of various objects depicted in a puzzle, she gave many wrong answers rather than saying she did not know: "This lack of attention . . . does not lead to impoverished testimony, but rather to testimony that contains many errors" (p. 30).

Most striking, however, is the Sterns' prescience regarding the developmental path from false suggestion that is apparent to a child to a deeply embedded unconscious error. In describing an instance in which their 28-month-old son Günter, on returning home, spontaneously and falsely reported having encountered a pair of friends during a trip to the park, the Sterns wrote, "Even among older children, and even among adults, it can happen that something that is at first elicited only by a leading question can gradually take on a spontaneous form and as such be evaluated psychologically as something other than what it is" (p. 70). Thus the Sterns drew the distinction referred to by contemporary developmentalists as that between *knowing* and *remembering* (Flavell, 1989).

When we wrote our review paper on the suggestibility of children for the *Psychological Bulletin* (Ceci & Bruck, 1993), and reviewed the historical work in our recent book (Ceci & Bruck, 1995), we summarized the findings of the pioneers (of which W. Stern was among the leaders) of suggestibility research as follows:

> This early work foreshadowed a large number of findings that were to appear in the modern literature, such as the idea that repeated questioning is detrimental, that questions are interpreted as "imperatives" by young children, requiring answers even if none is available, that free recall produces fewer errors than yes/no questioning, that a witness' confidence is often unrelated to accuracy, that fantasy–reality distinctions are problematic for very young children, and that even adults are suggestible to some degree. (Ceci & Bruck, 1995)

Unfortunately, when we wrote this we did not have available Lamiell's excellent translation of the Sterns' work. Future reviews of the historical literature are destined to include the major points discussed in this volume as well as a sincere acknowledgment to Lamiell for providing modern scholars with access to the intellectual foundations of their work.

# REFERENCES

Ceci, S. J., & Bruck, M. (1993). The suggestibility of the child witness: A historical review and synthesis. *Psychological Bulletin, 113,* 403–439.

Ceci, S. J., & Bruck, M. (1995). *Jeopardy in the courtroom: A scientific analysis of children's testimony.* Washington, DC: American Psychological Association.

Flavell, J. H. (1989). The development of children's knowledge about the mind. In J. W. Astington, P. L. Harris, & D. R. Olson (Eds.), *Developing theories of mind* (pp. 247–267). New York: Cambridge University Press.

Rovee-Collier, C. (1993). The capacity for long-term memory in infancy. *Current Directions in Psychological Science, 2,* 30–135.

# TRANSLATOR'S PREFACE

JAMES T. LAMIELL

To achieve an accurate, clear, and useful translation, it is always necessary to balance the desire for fidelity to the words of the original text against the requirement to produce a translation that is readable. This can be all the more challenging when the time gap between the publication of the original and the publication of the translation is as great as in the present case. Fortunately, the Sterns' writing style, although unmistakably scholarly, was also both clear and engaging, and these qualities eased the burden of translation considerably.

Still, there were contexts in which liberties had to be taken to effectively convey the meanings presumably intended by the authors. This was often necessary, for example, when dealing with "baby talk." There are many places in the original text in which the Sterns sought to represent phonetically the speech sounds being made by young children who had not yet mastered adult speech. Were this work directly concerned with language or speech per se, it would have been much more crucial to preserve in the translation the exact expressions given in the original text. Because speech is not the focus in this work, however, I chose to render instances of German baby talk in an appropriate English counterpart; this usually made a literal translation out of the question. An example may serve to clarify.

In chapter 4, the Sterns develop a point that entails reference to a well-known German-language children's verse that runs "*a, b, c, die Katze läuft im Schnee.*" For readers unfamiliar with German, this would be pronounced "ah, bay, tsay, dee Kahtzuh loyft im Shnay," with "tsay" and "Shnay" rhyming. The child's expression of this verse was rendered as "*a, b, c, da ja snee.*" But in English, the literal translation of the verse runs "a, b, c, the cat runs in the snow," and, quite obviously, this does not work! Therefore, I substituted for this passage the equally familiar and roughly comparable English language children's verse, "Hickory, dickory dock, the mouse ran up the clock" and I rendered the child's version of it as *"hicky, dicky, dock, mous uh clock."* In this fashion, I think, the central meaning of the original passage is preserved in a way that "works" in English.

Because the German word for "child," *das Kind*, is a neuter noun, the grammatically correct pronomial reference in German is *es*, or "it." In English, however, one does not refer to a child as "it." Accordingly, when context made obvious the gender of the child to which the Sterns were referring in some given instance, I have used either "he" or "she" as the pronomial reference. In other instances, the practice was followed of alternating between the two pronouns, striving for balance across the work as a whole.

The footnotes from the original text are presented in this volume as endnotes. It should be mentioned, however, that in the original text the Sterns followed a practice of numbering footnotes sequentially on a given page, but then reverting to number 1 to mark the first footnote appearing on a subsequent page. For example, the reader who would consult the original text would find footnotes numbered 1, 2, and 3 on p. 46, and then footnotes numbered 1 and 2 on p. 47. In contrast to this, the endnotes in the present text are numbered in one continuous sequence from the beginning to the end of the book. Therefore, the numbers accurately reflect the relative positioning of the footnotes in the original text, but no longer correspond to the original numbering. The reader is referred to the endnotes by the conventional superscripted numerals in the text.

Two additional points must be made regarding the endnotes. First, many of the footnotes in the original text served only the function of referring the reader to one or more titles in the bibliography at the end of the book. To avoid cumbersome cross-referencing, I have, whenever possible, converted the text to current APA-style name–date references and eliminated the corresponding endnote. However, all of the original footnotes that contained substantive commentary (rather than just a literature citation) have been retained as endnotes in the present work.

An additional point to be made is that some of the endnotes are translator's notes, which I have added in places where clarification or elaboration seemed necessary. All translator's notes are clearly identified as such.

The bibliography of the present volume reproduces the one provided by the Sterns in the original work, with the exception that English translations of titles have been added. I have done this even if no English translation of a given work is available, so that the reader can gain a sense for the content of the literature to which the Sterns referred in their work. Journal names and other points of information provided in the original have not been translated. However, if an English translation of a cited work does exist, the appropriate bibliographical information is provided.

The references section of this volume lists, in current APA format, works mentioned by the Sterns in the original but not listed in their bibliography, as well as publications that have been referenced in the Introduction coauthored by Werner Deutsch and myself. Here, too, English translations of titles have been provided, and bibliographical information for existing English translations of complete works has also been provided where appropriate.

In the main, this translation is my work. Fortunately, my colleague and friend Dr. Werner Deutsch of the Department of Developmental Psychology in the Psychological Institute of the Technical University of Braunschweig in Germany was willing to devote much time and effort to an examination of the text for fidelity to the original work and for clarity of the English rendition. As a native German speaker fluent in English and thoroughly familiar with the works of the Sterns, Dr. Deutsch was the ideal person for this difficult task, and I wish to record here my deep appreciation for his contribution. He has made it possible for me to sign off on this work in reasonable confidence that it does some measure of justice to the Sterns' original landmark contribution. Of course, I bear full responsibility for any flaws that remain.

There are several other individuals whom I would like to acknowledge for helping, in one way or another, to bring this project to fruition. First of all, I wish to thank the editors of the series in which this book appears, R. Bruce Sales, Stephen J. Ceci, and my Georgetown colleague Norman J. Finkel, for their faith in the project and their assistance in launching it. At APA Books, Julia Frank-McNeil and Susan Reynolds eased me over a variety of administrative hurdles, and development editor Judy Nemes made extremely valuable suggestions for improving the text and for the design of the book's cover. As project manager, Debbie Hardin contributed the sort of close and insightful copyediting for which any author or editor would be grateful.

In Berlin, I have spent many stimulating hours in discussions with Frank Radtke and Gerald Bühring, and through those discussions they have contributed greatly if indirectly to this undertaking. The same can be said of my Georgetown colleague Steven R. Sabat.

Portions of this project were completed early in 1998, when I was privileged to be Fulbright Senior Scholar to the University of Leipzig. I am grateful to Gitta Scheibler for her technical and clerical support, and to Siegfried Hoppe-Graff for his comraderie and collegiality during my months in Leipzig. In this connection, I would also like to express my gratitude to the members of the Fulbright Commission for Educational Exchange Between the United States and the Federal Republic of Germany for the opportunity they afforded me to do my work in an environment so well suited to it.

# INTRODUCTION

JAMES T. LAMIELL AND WERNER DEUTSCH

My dear friend,

   It has been so long since we have written to one another that I really don't know whose turn it is. I admit that, somewhere in the back of my mind I have a certain feeling of guilt, but it is rather minimized by the fact that during the past four months I have quite naturally been greatly absorbed in my new role as a father. And if you could see our sweet little Hilde, you would understand why her father scarcely has time for anything else, even for a letter to an old friend . . .

—Letter from William Stern to the Friedburg philosopher Jonas Cohn
July 31, 1900

On the day that "sweet little Hilde" was born to Clara Stern (1878–1945) and husband William (1871–1938), William made the following entry in a diary:

Born April 7, 1900, 2:00 a.m.
Observations before birth:
   First movements were sensed around mid (13th?) Oct.
   The movements were always more lively [when mother] in the bath.
First day, 7 April
   Birth followed 24-hour labor. When only the head had appeared and the child's eyes were wiped with cold water, she grimaced as if to cry. First cry as the baby had completely emerged with the exception of one foot.
   When laid on the table, she immediately sucked her thumb. An

"*aayhaay*" was clear in the cry of the first day, the "*aay*" sound inclining somewhat to "*ay*," especially the second.

The *h* unmistakably clear.

Almost all cries had this form.

Immediately following birth the child reacted neither to sounds (hands clapping) nor to light (gas flame). On the other hand, at 5 hours of age she seemed to react to mother's short, sharp "*shhhh*," by twice immediately suppressing her crying.

In the evening she was placed at the left breast and after a few seconds began to make the sucking movements correctly.

The work begun with these lines eventually would grow in volume to roughly 5000 handwritten pages, extend in time over some 18 years, and preserve for posterity extensive observations on the development not only of Hilde but also of son Günther (born in 1902) and second daughter Eva (born in 1904). By no means were the Sterns the first to systematically record observations of children for subsequent analysis and discussion by scholars and other interested professionals. For example, Dietrich Tiedemann had published his *Observations on the Development of the Mental Abilities of Children* well more than a century earlier, in 1787, and other similar works appeared shortly before that of the Sterns (e.g., books by Preyer in 1888 and by Sully in 1895 [German translation 1897]). In terms of their thoroughness and breadth, however, the Stern diaries would eventually outpace all other works of their kind. In a general reference to the works, William Stern would later write,

> In a fashion not constrained by some preestablished framework, the psychological development of three very different children from birth until well into the school years was recorded in these diaries.... What was eventually published—some of it by my wife and me together, some by me alone—reflects only in a limited way the richness and breadth of the material.

From that material, the Sterns originally planned to produce six "Monographs on the Psychological Development of the Child." The topics on which they planned to write included (a) child language; (b) recollection, testimony, and lying in early childhood; (c) observing and portraying; (d) child play; (e) the life of the will and emotions; and (f) thinking and world view. As it would happen, only the first two of these six planned monographs were ever published: *Die Kindersprache (Children's Speech)* appeared in 1907, and *Erinnerung, Aussage, und Lüge in der ersten Kindheit (Recollection, Testimony, and Lying in Early Childhood)* appeared two years later. Until now, neither of these two works has ever been available in its entirety in English.

Our goal in this introductory chapter is in part to provide the reader with a glimpse into the contents of *Recollection, Testimony, and Lying in Early Childhood*. Beyond this, however, we also hope to give the reader a sense of the larger context in which this work emerged and with respect to which its contemporary significance can be judged. We will conclude with some brief remarks pertaining to the translation.

## PRELIMINARY OVERVIEW

For both theoretical and practical reasons, many child psychologists, pedagogues, legal professionals, and others have long sought to understand more fully the extent to which young children are able to recall their experiences and to report on them accurately. As part of this effort, there has also been a great interest in learning more about the developmental course through which young children acquire the capacity—and, in some cases, the inclination—to lie. As important as these topics are, and as extensive as the interest in them is, the fact that until now no English-language translation of Clara and William Stern's truly pathbreaking work has been available is certainly a large part of the reason that few contemporary scholars, researchers, or practitioners are familiar with its contents. Those contents remain highly relevant to contemporary thinking on the subject, even as the century that was in its infancy when this work was originally published draws to its close.

Part I of the book, consisting of the work's first three chapters, is essentially a case study in which the Sterns rely on diary entries made for Hilde over the first 7 or so years of her life; this will introduce the reader to relevant topics. Beginning with a distinction by now familiar to every student of cognition and memory, that between *recognition* (*das Wiedererkennen*) and *recall* (*die Erinnerung*), the Sterns note that, from a developmental standpoint, the former is the foundation for the latter. They proceed to discuss the chronological development of recall and of testimonial ability, and then turn to a consideration of false testimony. In this latter regard, crucial distinctions are drawn between *genuine lies* (*Lügen*) on the one hand and both *mistaken recollections* (*Erinnerungstäuschungen*) and *pseudo-lies* (*Scheinlügen*) on the other. All of the empirical data introduced in Part I pertain to a single research "subject": the Sterns' daughter Hilde.

In Part II, made up of chapters 4 through 10, the authors bring into consideration, in comparative fashion, diary entries they had made based on observations of Günther (born in 1902) and of Eva (born in 1904). Relevant observations that had been reported in the literature up to that time by other investigators are also considered throughout the various chapters of this section. Beyond the previously noted works by Tiedemann, Preyer, and Sully, contributions by many other scholars—among them Ament, Binet, Dürr-Borst, Compayré, Groos, Hall, Lindner, Major, Rousseau, and Scupin—are mentioned. It is also in this section of the book that the Sterns present the empirical results of some systematic experiments that they carried out—very carefully and unobtrusively—with their three children. The specific topics discussed in this part of the book overlap with those that had been considered in the first part: recognition, purposive recollections, correct recollections, and mistaken recollections. The discussion of lying treats not only genuine lies but also "pseudo lies" and the sometimes falsifying effects of fantasy. The Sterns briefly discuss what might be considered the opposite of problematic lying: "truth fanaticism."

In Part III, the Sterns consider the practical implications of their research findings. They discuss concrete ways in which parents and others entrusted with the rearing of children can train young persons to observe things accurately in the first instance, and then report accurately on what they have experienced. They draw attention to the importance of allowing children to discover on their own such mistakes as they may have made in giving testimony about some or other occurrence, and they caution parents and caregivers against drawing hasty conclusions about whether a child who has told an *untruth* has in fact *lied.* They discuss further the origins of lying and its prevention and, finally, they present their views on the capacities—and limitations—of small children as witnesses in legal proceedings. In this latter context, they offer guidelines indicating how children should and should not be interrogated in connection with legal proceedings.

## VIEWING THE STERNS' CONTRIBUTIONS IN LIGHT OF CONTEMPORARY DEVELOPMENTAL PSYCHOLOGY

When the Sterns planned, prepared, and wrote this monograph more than 90 years ago, the topic of memory development in children was still *terra incognita.* The Sterns were fortunate to be in the position of pioneers. The scientific luggage with which they journeyed consisted of hundreds of pages of diary entries that they had made based on observations of their three children. The Sterns were able to determine for themselves the theoretical framework of their project and the methodological approach they would take. It is striking how little notice they took of the experimental psychology of memory that would subsequently blossom. After all, William Stern had studied under Hermann Ebbinghaus, whose experimental investigations into the learning and recollection of lists of nonsense syllables became the model for memory research as that area of inquiry has developed up to present time.

One reason that suggests itself as an explanation for the distance between the Sterns' work and the psychology of memory as Ebbinghaus saw it is that, for the Sterns, the observation of the experiences and behaviors of *persons* in their *natural milieus* constituted the appropriate point of departure for their entire developmental psychology. To the greatest extent possible, such observations would best be made not in the laboratory, under highly artificial conditions, but rather in the places in which the children actually lived. Thanks to their diary recordings, the Sterns were able to trace the developmentally specific regularities of the psychology of memory without having to limit from the outset the form and content of the phenomena under investigation through the imposition of particular experimental procedures or psychological tests. The Sterns proceeded from a functional view of memory. The impressions gained by Person A at time $t(1)$ could have subsequent effects and be reexperienced at time $t(2)$. Distinctions could be drawn between different kinds of effects. When a child has met another person for the first time, the second meeting might lead to the experience of recognition. This recognition might, for example, be discernable from the child's facial expression, even if the child could not name the person who has been recognized. What is the role of the length of the $t(1) - t(2)$ interval in the child's ability to have such an experience of recognition? With their diary entries, the Sterns possessed a database suited to the task of gaining answers to such questions that would be informative from the standpoint of developmental psychology. It turns out that the temporal interval in question is not a single, generally valid constant, but is itself subject to developmentally specific changes.

When she was 12 months old, Hilde could recognize her father after a 14-day separation. At the age of 27 months, Hilde was able to recognize her grandmother after three months had elapsed since the previous meeting. Finally, at the age of 3 years and 1 month, Hilde recognized her aunt after a separation of seven months. The observations of this specific case make clear something that is also found in other children: Recognition is the first memoric function that emerges in development.

What changes in the course of development is the magnitude of the time interval $t(1) - t(2)$, an interval the Sterns labeled *latency time*. Nor is this the only law-like regularity that the Sterns were able to uncover through their developmentally specific analyses. In the first and second years of life recognition is only possible when that which is recognized— at first persons and objects, later the spatial and physical environment— actually reappears. From the beginning of the third year of life on, recognition is possible when that which is recognized occurs only occasionally, or even only once. In this latter case, not just any old impression will be recalled, but rather only those that are affectively charged, such as an unpleasant visit to the doctor or a trip that entails many disruptive changes in location, daily schedule, and so on.

After recognition, the second function of memory is that of *recollection*. This function appears gradually, passing through four major developmental stages. The first stage is one characterized by associative connections, through which a present sense impression is related to a previous one. The second stage is characterized by freestanding recollections, which surface in consciousness suddenly and with no obvious prompting. In contrast with these first two stages, in which recollections arise on their own, as it were, the third stage entails recollections that are prompted from without—for example, through questioning or in the course of a legal hearing. As the Sterns demonstrated in small-scale experiments carried out with their children, such provoked recollections are especially susceptible to mistakes, whereby something is said to have been experienced, though in reality it did not happen. The Sterns argue that these mistaken recollections are not intentional untruths. The more leading the questions are that are put to children (or, for that matter, adults), the more frequent is the occurrence of mistaken recollections.

The fourth stage, that of intentional recollection, entails a decision to take note of something or to bring it to mind. During the preschool years recollections of this sort are rare, because the playful aspects of memory have priority over the intentional recollection of things that have been learned, which is required in school.

The forms of memory develop in the sequence just described. However, it is not only the forms but also the contents of recollections that follow a lawful developmental sequence. Early on, recollections for things that have been experienced *visually* dominate, whereas recollections for *linguistic–acoustic* experiences occur later. It is not until the child has reached the age of about 3 years that these latter sorts of experiences play an important role. This comes to be the case, for example, when children repeat many verses or songs without understanding their content.

In the Sterns' view, recollections come to be bound to mental images or ideas, so that in the course of development, memory is increasingly independent of direct perception. How can the existence of such mental images in development be proven? On this question, too, the Sterns did truly pioneering work: They discovered and drew attention to the developing inclination of children to seek out objects that had disappeared (i.e., were no longer visible to the child), and they used this behavioral indicator as evidence for the existence of mental images. This same developmental achievement is something Piaget later called *object permanence*.

Much that the Sterns discovered in their work has, in the intervening 90 years, gradually found a way into textbook treatments of memory development. Beyond the example of object permanence just mentioned, also note (a) the appearance–reality distinction, (b) the existence of meta-memory, (c) the difference between semantic and episodic memory, (d) what is now called *implicit memory*—in other words, memory for experiences one cannot recall having had, and (e) the anticipation of *theory of mind* research in relation to lying. One searches the literature in vain for instances in which the rediscoverers of these phenomena mention the names of the original discoverers. It is not easy to explain away the fact that the pioneering work of the Sterns has been so seldom read—let alone properly acknowledged—on the grounds that no English-language renditions of the relevant work has been available, because an English translation of the developmental psychology textbook authored by William Stern, *The Psychology of Early Childhood*, has been available for decades.

There can be little doubt about the propriety of regarding *Erinnerung, Aussage und Lüge in der ersten Kindheit* as a truly *signal* contribution to developmental psychology in general, and to our understanding of children's psychological capacities and limitations in the context of legal proceedings in particular. For these reasons alone, the publication of an English translation of the work is warranted. However, there is much more to recommend the project.

In making their discoveries, the Sterns relied on a method—the diary method—through which developmental psychology was scientifically enriched. Yet this very method fell into discredit while the Sterns were still living, and it is arguable that developmental psychology is suffering the untoward consequences of this up to the present day. We may ask, since the time of the Sterns, who among those investigators professing an interest in the development of memory has studied individual children in longitudinal fashion to document the developmental course of children's memory functions in a way that would even approximate the comprehensiveness achieved by the Sterns, and then has tested hypotheses concerning the general lawfulness of certain phenomena? The answer, of course, is no one. Nor is the explanation for this simply that a certain method fell into disfavor, for such things do not happen accidentally. On the contrary, within mainstream scientific psychology in general, the person-centered perspective—a perspective obviously compatible with the diary method—fell into disfavor or, perhaps better said, never really enjoyed widespread favor to begin with. Yet this was very much the perspective that grounded the Sterns' work, and in the interest of achieving a fuller appreciation for the fruits of their labor, it is worth it to consider briefly some of the major features of that perspective.

## CRITICAL PERSONALISM: THE CONCEPTUAL FOUNDATIONS OF THE STERNS' WORK

In an intellectual autobiography (*Selbstdarstellung*) published nearly 20 years after the appearance in 1909 of *Recollection, Testimony, and Lying in Early Childhood* in 1909, William Stern wrote,

> For my own scientific development, the studies of my own children were significant in yet another way. Here I observed psychological life concretely, and in this way I was protected from those ivory-tower schemes and abstractions that we all too often encounter in the name of psychology. It was through this work that I came to understand the

person as the center of a *unitas multiplex*. That is, I came to see how a great multiplicity of psychological contents can exist within a single individual, either simultaneously or sequentially, and yet all converge on that developing person's unitary life line, thus endowing the multifaceted psychological contents of a life with meaning. The diary material impressed on me the fundamental form of personal causality, which is the convergence of the propensities present in a child with the totality of outer influences. In short, the diary material provided me with a perspectival foundation for the philosophical theory I was gradually developing. (Stern, 1927, p. 17)

The philosophical theory Stern mentioned is a system of thought he called *critical personalism*. The fullness of William Stern's ideas concerning this system required three separate volumes to convey, and these appeared over nearly two decades: *Philosophical Foundations*, the first volume of *Person and Thing: A Systematic Philosophical World View*, was published in 1906 (3 years prior to the appearance of *Recollection, Testimony, and Lying in Early Childhood*). Volume 2 of *Person and Thing* appeared in 1918, and was titled *The Human Personality*. Volume 3 was published in 1924 as *Philosophy of Values*, and with the publication of this volume Stern altered the series title slightly to *Person and Thing: The System of Critical Personalism*.

Through its very name, *critical personalism*, William Stern intended to distinguish his *Weltanschauung* both from *naive personalism*, a view that accepts uncritically a mind–body dualism Stern hoped to circumvent, and also—more so—from *im*personalism—in other words, an utterly mechanistic standpoint according to which, in Stern's view, persons are simply reduced to things. The importance of this last point cannot be exaggerated, for as his series title suggests, the distinction between persons and things was absolutely fundamental to William Stern's entire outlook. A full appreciation of his many works—including but not limited to this one— requires that this be kept firmly in mind.

"A person," Stern claimed, "is an entity that, though comprised of many parts, fashions a genuine, unique unity, is intrinsically valuable, and as such, is the source of its own unitary, goal-oriented activity notwithstanding the multiplicity of its various part-functions. A thing, " in contrast, "is an entity that, while also consisting of many parts, does not fashion any genuine or unique unity of intrinsic value, and is thus an entity that, though it functions in accordance with its many parts, is never the source of its own unitary, goal-oriented activity" (Stern, 1924, p. 66).

Already in Volume 1 of *Person and Thing*, Stern had highlighted his thoroughly nonmechanistic conception of human persons:

The impersonal natural philosopher sits at his desk and writes, "What we call a human is, physically, nothing but an aggregate of atoms or, as the case may be, energy quanta, and, psychologically, nothing but an aggregate of consciousness contents. Nothing happens except that which must occur as a consequence of the blind causal relationship of physical elements. And the person's so-called psychological life is nothing but the mechanical coupling of those physical elements." But then he steps into the nursery, where his child is lying ill. He braces himself against the thought of losing this beloved being— beloved being? What is it about atom + atom + atom (or energy + energy + energy) and idea + idea + idea that merits love? And: lose? In one case (that of the so-called living individual) the elements are bound more tightly to one another; in the other instance they stand in looser relationship. In the former instance, the influx and outflow of energy is equal, in the latter case it is not. How can this entirely indifferent variability of purely spacial constellation or energy flow mean the difference between joy and despair? And if his other child comes home from school with poor grades, he warns the child: "You should do better." Better? Is there a better or a worse in the indifferent coupling of indifferent atoms and indifferent ideas? Whence this scale of values all of a sudden? Whence values at all? And: You should? Where mechanical laws and nothing else are at work, how can there be such a thing as "should"? Because "should" signifies nothing other than the determination of one's own doings through the consciousness of a goal. "Should" is something that can exist only for a self-activated being, a mere string of elements cannot "should." (Stern, 1906, p. 79)

In the aforementioned intellectual biography, Stern (1927) indicated that his overriding, life-long scholarly concern was the question of how to conceive of human individuality in a way that would prove both philosophically sound and scientifically valid. When all is said and done, critical personalism is the answer to this question that Stern gradually worked out over the course of his highly productive professional life.

We have already seen that Stern regarded a clear distinction between *persons* and *things* as fundamental. Even some years before 1900 he was becoming worried that the mainstream experimental psychology of the time—in other words, the psychology of such luminaries as Wilhelm Wundt and Stern's own teacher—and eventually senior colleague Hermann Ebbinghaus—was moving inexorably in a direction that would blur and ultimately obliterate that distinction. This is the concern that gave impetus to the major scholarly project of his life: critical personalism. No adequate recapitulation of that project here would be possible, nor is that necessary. Our objective is merely to draw attention to the fact that, as a developing system of thought, critical personalism was underway by the time of daughter Hilde's birth in 1900, and there is no question that William Stern's thinking about the nature of human persons and, in turn, the "fabric" of the larger social–moral order, helped to guide and was in its turn nourished by the multifaceted diary observations of Hilde, Günther, and Eva on which *Recollection, Testimony, and Lying in Early Childhood* was based. Moreover, critical personalism, as it had been developed by 1909, undoubtedly influenced both the structure and the content that Clara and William Stern gave to the book itself.

## The Person-Centered Approach to Psychological Investigation

As the Sterns open Part I of the text, they note that critics of single-case studies have argued against the scientific utility of such works on the grounds that their findings cannot be generalized. What the Sterns hasten to point out, however, is that absent some close examination of the individual case, there is no way to know which questions to pursue in quest of knowledge that is generalizable. It is not difficult to see how this view is reflected in the book's overall structure. One properly begins, the Sterns contend, with the systematic and detailed study of an individual case. Subsequently, one can—indeed one should—investigate the extent to which specific empirical findings do and do not hold up across additional individual cases and hence may or may not properly be regarded as *generally* valid in the sense of *allen gemein: common to all* of those individual cases. Note that even as investigation proceeds into this second phase, it does not abandon the "$N = 1$" approach but instead *repeats* it. This, then, is the larger design of the present work, and it may be seen as a reflection of the (critically) personalistic outlook to which William Stern was committed.

## Intentionality as a Fundamental Aspect of Human Psychological Functioning

Of course, commitment to the study of persons does not, by itself, constitute a system of thought. One must immediately embrace some sort of a conception of persons as a way of initiating and guiding subsequent inquiry. Rudimentary to Stern's view, as we have already seen from his definition of a person, is a teleological outlook: The person is seen as irreducibly self-directed and goal-striving—in other words, *intentional*. One particularly instructive illustration of this outlook is found in chapter 2. The authors are discussing what they call the *latency interval*, the interval of time that a child can successfully bridge between an experience and its subsequent recall. What is noteworthy in this context, the Sterns write, "is that the extension backward (into the past) occurs later than does the extension forward. . . . At a time when the child still cannot report on something that has just happened, the immediate future is already an object of expressions. . . . As an intentional being, the child wants something much sooner than it confirms something" (from original text; see p. 10 of this volume).

Of course, intentionality is of crucial relevance to the entire question of lying, one of the major topics of this work. For even if a child knows that something she or he is saying is false but has no intention of deceiving, there can be no genuine lie. The requisite intention is clearly lacking when the child is engaged in fantasy play, but the Sterns argue that it is also lacking when a child's knowingly untruthful utterances are serving an essentially defensive function. The discussion in chapter 10 of pseudo-lies develops this point in detail.

### The Principle of Convergence

The fact that persons are genuinely (and not just apparently) intentional beings—and hence are capable of exercising their will—does not mean that they are always and everywhere free to do entirely as they please. There exist constraints, some of which are imposed by the human being's very physical–biological nature, and some of which are imposed by the external environment—social as well as physical. Within the framework of critical personalism, an account of the role that these factors play in the production of behavior is achieved through what William Stern called *convergence*: The individual person's purposes or objectives are realized (or at least sought) through actions that accommodate the constraints imposed by one's own physical limits or the outer—physical and social—world. In this work, the reader will find many concrete examples of convergence, but one simple instructive illustration of convergence with the physical environment is provided by the Sterns' discussion of Hilde's attempt to convey her understanding of certain spatial relations.

During a conversation with Hilde about a long-past visit to the city of Jannowitz, Hilde was asked to talk about where various members of the family had been quartered. The Sterns describe how at the age of 3 years and 7 months Hilde used the table top to describe the relative spatial locations of the different bedrooms. "The observations," the Sterns note, "show how little recollection has to do with absolute size; how basic, on the other hand, is the tendency and the capability to project unvisualisable dimensions of size and distance into the framework of what is visually possible" (from the original text; see p. 17 of this volume).

### Intentionality, Human Values, and Critical Personalism's Social–Ethical Conception of Community

It was noted previously in the introduction of *convergence* that biological and environmental factors constrain the behavior of persons in various ways. Beyond this, however, and in ways that are ultimately of even greater significance, critical personalism views the behavior of individuals as being necessarily and hence properly constrained by those human values necessary to sustain a larger social–moral order.

In the vocabulary of critical personalism, and in a way reflective of the aforementioned commitment by William Stern to a fundamentally teleological conception of the human condition, *autotelie* is a word he used to refer to the intentions of the individual (autonomous) person. In like fashion, however, Stern used the term *heterotelie* to help capture the fact that individuals live within a heterogeneous interpersonal world constituted (in part) of higher order social units with their own goals and values. These considerations provided Stern with a basis for his conception of *community*:

> (One) who pursues only his/her own narrow individual goals (*autotelie*) would be an extensionless point in emptiness. Only the goals extending beyond the self give the person concrete content and living coherence with the world. The *heterotelie* emerges over against the autotelie. . . . Each person is a member of higher unities, which for their part have the character of living wholes (personalities in the larger sense) with their own goals . . . family, folk, humanity, deity. Partaking in these higher unities signifies for the individual a serviceability with respect to their goals: [this is] *hypertelie* . . . It is a fact not to be analyzed further, perhaps the last and highest secret of the human personality, that it takes up the heterotelic into the autotelic. The outer goal indeed remains, after as before, directed to the not-I, but it is appropriated within and formed according to one's own self. Only in this way does it become possible that the surrender to supra-personal and nonpersonal goals nevertheless does not signify any de-personalization, or any degradation of the personality into a mere thing and tool, but that, on the contrary, the personality becomes, through its embodiment of the outer goals in its self activity, a microcosmos. (Stern, 1917, pp. 46–47)

It is not surprising that it is in those places in which the Sterns are addressing themselves to some aspect of lying that this work reflects most vividly the notions expressed in the previous passage. Throughout the book, it is obvious how much importance Clara and William Stern—as parents—placed on truthfulness in their own child-rearing practices. Beyond this, however, the Sterns were careful to point out the responsibility that parents and other adults entrusted with child-rearing have, both to implement practices that will nurture truth telling by children and to avoid practices that will undermine this objective.

The Sterns believed that children are not naturally inclined toward lying. They do, however, have other natural inclinations that parents and other child-rearers can wittingly or unwittingly exploit or damage in ways that can result in more or less chronic lying. This eventuality, of course, is detrimental to the social fabric, and that is what makes it problematic. In reading what the Sterns have to say on this topic, many contemporary readers will find ample reason to reflect critically on their own practices with children and those of other adults in their acquaintance.

Along these lines but carrying implications extending well beyond the topic of lying per se, it should be noted that although critical personalism is ever respectful of human individuality, it is *not* fertile philosophical soil for an excessive individualism. On the contrary, the person whose individuality would be nurtured by the community has in turn the positive moral duty to contribute to the integrity of that very community. This calls in turn for child-rearing practices that will facilitate the realization of that objective, and any recommendations that would run contrary to this tenet would have to be rejected, according to the Sterns. The consistency of this view with a central tenet of critical personalism is unmistakable. In the introduction to his *The Human Personality*, William Stern described critical personalism as a system of thought.

> as distant from a one-sided individualism recognizing only the right and happiness of the single individual as from a socialism in which individual uniqueness and personal freedom are choked by the pressure of supra-personal demands. (1918, p. XI)

It is arguably among the more unfortunate developments in twentieth-century psychology that Stern's critical personalism has never been especially prominent or widely discussed as a framework for psychological research and theorizing (Deutsch, 1991; Lamiell, 1996). With this is mind, we invite the reader to consider *Recollection, Testimony and Lying in Early Childhood* not only as the important contribution to developmental psychology and to psychology and law that it surely is but also as a vivid example of the kind of psychological inquiry to which critical personalism can lead. This might well help to spark renewed interest in a system of thought whose time, perhaps, has finally come.

# FOREWORD TO THE ORIGINAL VOLUME

CLARA AND WILLIAM STERN

To date, research in child psychology has concentrated mainly on the first years of life and on the school years. In most instances, investigations in the first category have been carried out by members of the child's family, whereas those in the second category have usually been conducted by professional pedagogues. Our monographs concern the preschool child. However, we do not limit ourselves to the first 3 years, as have most others following Preyer's (1888) example. Instead, we include in our considerations the remaining preschool years, to the extent that the problems under consideration demand this and to the degree that the available materials allow it.

Our investigations are based on records that we have made of our own children (Hilde, born April 7, 1900; Günther, born July 12, 1902; and Eva, born December 29, 1904). In this work, we did not need to adhere to a preestablished observational scheme—as, for example, Preyer did by undertaking to make observations of his son at specific times of the day. The reason for this is that life in the nursery, with all of its pleasures and pains, all of its routine and special occasions, was occurring around the parents, and more specifically around the mother, all the time, and thus offered countless opportunities to follow and to pinpoint the psychological development of the young person in a wide variety of respects, including language, play, will and character, intelligence, emotion, perception, artistic activity, and so forth. This project entailed continuous collaboration on the part of the parents, and this proved helpful for us to see how the various domains are interrelated, how to formulate the problems for investigation, and how to analyze the material.

Our method was the following: Where the focus was not on a literal recording of speech utterances, the observations were recorded or noted in a preliminary fashion, so that in the evening they could be entered more thoroughly in the diaries. If a word-for-word record was needed, then of course the necessary record was made immediately, sometimes with the aid of stenography.

Throughout our investigations, we were able to disguise our procedure. Up to now, our eldest daughter, 9-year-old Hilde, has no idea that a written record of her and her siblings is being kept. This seems to us absolutely essential. First, the procedure protects against untoward influences on the character of the children. Second, it helps us to capture the children's various expressions and behaviors in their genuine, childish innocence.

Only rarely did we resort to experiments, and then only in ways that were engaging to the child. To this end, pictures proved very helpful to us in many connections, as means of testing perception, testimony, intelligence, and speech. Tiring experiments—for example, on color recognition, learning to count, and so forth—were things we avoided, not just because such procedures are only burdensome to the children, but also because we did not wish to artificially hasten or otherwise alter the natural course of development.

Because our raw material has been recorded chronologically and separately for each child, it contains a kind of psychological biography of the children. However, we decided against publishing the material in this form, because the continuous jumping from one to another content area of observation would confuse rather than enlighten the reader. So we regarded a monographic treatment as necessary, because only the focus on a selected developing function permits an exhaustive and comprehensive investigation. In this regard, we are well aware that discussing various functions separately is to some extent artificial, and that, for example, the development of speech or of play or perception can be fully understood only within the context of the overall psychological development of the child. Therefore, throughout this work we have sought to refer repeatedly to the general "psycho-genetic" viewpoint.[1,2]

The isolation of specific problems also makes it possible to go beyond the respective developments of our own children and to refer to the extant literature for purposes of comparison. In this way it was possible to separate those aspects of development that were generally valid from those that are differentially valid. Finally, it was also possible to consider, to the extent

---

[1] Translator's note: By "psycho-genetic" viewpoint, the Sterns mean to refer to the developmental emergence of various psychological phenomena.
[2] In this regard, the essay by W. Stern titled, "Facts and Causes of Psychological Development" (*Zeitschrift für angewandte Psychologie und psychologische Sammelforschung*, 1907, *1*, 1–43) may be regarded as an introduction to these monographs.

possible, the parallels that exist between the psychological development of the child and that of humankind.

An important factor in the biographical portrayal of a child is the reporting of age, and this is a matter that heretofore has been handled idiosyncratically in the literature. Almost every child psychologist has his or her own system. An age of 2 years and 10 months is recorded by one as 1030 days, by another as 34 months, and by a third as "in the twelfth quarter-year." A fourth investigator has even reported "III,4,4" (that is, in the fourth weeks of the fourth quarter of the third year). The reader is always faced anew with a recording system that is, at best, burdensome.

In these monographs we use a system for reporting age that, in consideration of its simplicity, we would like to recommend for general use. Years and months are shown separated by a semicolon. The month shown is not the current one but instead the last fully completed one (just as, for example, a timetable does not indicate one half to 5 but instead 4:30). So, for example, 2;10 means after 2 years 10 months, not, for example, in the tenth month of the second year. This system matches the customary way of talking: "the 2 yr. 10-month-old child," so that no more translation is necessary. Finer specifications of time are not necessary for most problems in child psychology, but in instances in which they are necessary, either a fraction of a month can be indicated (for example, 2;$10\frac{1}{2}$ = 2 years ten-and-one-half months), or one can put the extra days in parentheses: 2;10(5) = 2 years, ten months and 5 days. From time to time, the system requires a zero; for example, 0;5 = 5 months of age; 2;$0\frac{1}{2}$ = 2 years and $\frac{1}{2}$ month.

All age designations coming from other sources have been transcribed into our system.

The literal expressions of the children are shown in *italic* type. With regard to orthography, it is to be noted that for sound complexes that deviated from actual adult speech, we used letter combinations that would fit the sounds that the children were making (whereby we, as nonprofessionals, had to dispense with the diacritical fine points). Speech utterances of the children that concurred with mature speech are recorded in the conventional way.

We currently plan several monographs, quite varied in their scope. Over the course of several years, we hope to treat, separately, the following themes: child speech; recollection, testimony and lying; perception and portrayal; child play; the life of the will and emotions; thinking and world view.

Breslau, April 29, 1907 (November 1908)

# PREFACE TO THE ORIGINAL VOLUME

CLARA AND WILLIAM STERN

Recent studies of testimony, which began with adults and were then extended to children, need to be supplemented by studies of still younger children. The real development of the phenomena of relevance begins in the first years of life. The study of this age period is therefore indispensable for a theoretical understanding. From a practical standpoint, too, day care centers and kindergartens must deal with the problems of testimony and lying when children are still preschoolers.

Though previous investigators of children have contributed occasional observations on this matter, there is still a lack of a comprehensive investigation. It is hoped that this monograph will help to fill this gap. It covers the first 6 years of the psychological life of the normal child, but at times also covers material extending beyond this age limit.

To the extent that a child's testimony is correct, it constitutes a positive achievement, and we wish to trace this development step by step. To the extent that such testimony is false, the multifaceted psychological causes of this are of interest. The major difference consists of the absence or presence of the will to make false statements. For this reason, it is necessary to consider recollective illusions and effects of suggestion as well as confabulation and conscious lying.

Perception and observation, the precursors to recollection, are subjects that we have not covered as thoroughly as our material would allow. However, these are topics that will be treated later in a separate monograph.

The book is organized in three parts: a psychographic, a general–psychological, and an applied psychological part. The first part describes, in chronological order, the individual development of our oldest daughter's ability to report on what she has experienced—in other words, to *testify*. It is an expansion and partial reworking of the essay, "Recollection and Testimony in Early Childhood: A Chapter From the Psychological Development of a Child." This work appeared in *Contributions to the Psychology of Testimony* (1905, pp. 161–197).

In the second part of the work we consider for comparative purposes material that can be found in the currently available literature, as well as diary entries we have made of our two other children. We use this material, insofar as is possible, as the basis for a generalization of our findings. In this respect, it should be noted that we have had to restrict ourselves to children from the educated classes, because exact observations of working-class children are still not available.

The third part of this book offers practical and useful applications for early educational approaches to the issues of testimony and lying, as well as for dealing with small children in legal hearings.

At the end of the book is a bibliography, which is not limited to literature dealing with early childhood but includes as well the entire literature on testimony and lying in adolescence.

To those parents who so generously contributed to the expansion of certain key points through private correspondence we express our thanks.

As was the first monograph in this series, so too is this one—in the preliminary work as well as in the actual writing of the text—the result of our thoroughly collaborative effort.

Breslau, November 1908

# I

## INDIVIDUAL DEVELOPMENT OF THE ABILITY TO TESTIFY

In opposition to the method of portraying the individual in child psychology, critics have often maintained that the results of such investigations are not scientifically useful, because the findings obtained with a single child cannot be generalized. This view, however, overlooks an important use of child *psychography*—in other words, psychological studies of individual children over time—because the very issues warranting psychological investigation cannot be regarded as if they were somehow obvious from the start. On the contrary, the issues themselves emerge in their fullness only if one continuously follows the course of development of a particular individual. Moreover, the conditions giving rise to a specific phenomenon—in our case *testimony*, or the giving of some sort of report about something that has in some way been experienced—are probed quite differently when one studies individuals than when one studies large groups, in which any given individual is tested and observed only on an *ad hoc* basis. Both methods thus complement one another. Here, then, we offer the psychographic presentation of an individual child, and through this seek to identify the major issues to be pursued later from a comparative perspective.

Out of the developmental history of our daughter Hilde, who may be regarded as an altogether normal child, we select first the most primitive function of memory—in other words, recognition—and consider subsequently the achievements of recall as they become more advanced. Finally, we consider the false testimonies. We should acknowledge something that, although it is to us a source of great personal pleasure, might nevertheless indicate a deficiency in the objective record that our psychographic investigation has yielded: In Hilde's case, a genuine lie has yet to be observed up to the 9th year of age (the time of the appearance of this book).

Some of the experimental studies of testimony that we made of Hilde with the intention of comparing her later with her siblings are discussed not in the psychographic section of the book, but only later (in chapter 8).

As another point of clarification: By the expression *latency time*, we mean the time gap over which something can be recognized or recollected without any reminders during the interim.

# 1

# RECOGNITION AS THE BASIS
# OF RECOLLECTION

A child's first recognition is manifested simply by the fact that he or she greets as familiar what is being perceived at a given moment. The very young child is still entirely a creature of the present. A previously formed impression has an effect, but only "beneath the surface," so to speak. The impression still has not been formulated into an isolated content of consciousness (reproduction), but instead it lends to the child's current perception an altered nuance of feeling (the "being familiar" quality discussed by Höffding). Recognition in this primitive sense begins very early: The infant only a few months old already smiles at her mother, whose impression is familiar to the child. Soon the child "recognizes" all of the persons in her environment, as well as many objects; and the first instances of naming objects are manifestations of the child's ability to recognized things.

It is not necessary for us to discuss in detail these very primitive stages of recognition, because they have already been discussed by other authors.[1] Our central interest is in the child at that stage of development in which acts of recognition occur after longer and more readily measurable time intervals. The following material is presented in chronological order.

1;0 After her first trip to Berlin the 1-year-old child recognized father, from whom she had been separated for 14 days.[2] In the first moment when she saw him, she seemed estranged, but soon thereafter she was as at ease as before. At the time, we were unable to detect any sign that Hilde recognized the rooms of our apartment.

**1;5½**  After a 6-week trip during the summer, we noted the following of the nearly 1½-year-old child: "When Hilde entered the bedroom in the arms of her father, she looked around for a long time, staring without making a sound; we could not avoid the impression that things were gradually dawning on her. Hardly had she been placed into the little bed from which she had been absent for so long than she began to vocalize happily, and we in turn had to suspect that her beautiful bed seemed intimately familiar to her and prompted tumultuous pleasure. . . . When mother laid the child on the changing table soon after arriving home, she immediately reached, as she had always done prior to the trip, for the children's picture hanging on the wall, and pulled it down to play with it. It was not at all novel to her. The familiarity of the overall situation immediately set off once again, reflex-like, the grasping that had not occurred for 6 weeks. In another room, when Hilde first reencountered the grand piano, she stopped suddenly, sang 'lala,' and struck the keyboard cover. Hilde at first acted shy, quiet, and anxious toward her nanny, who had returned home 14 days earlier. She tried to get away from the nanny and go to her mother, but gradually the spell was broken. After about an hour, the child was playing with the nanny as if they had never been apart, and the two of them even went for a walk together."

**1;6**  The child of 1½ years immediately recognized her mother after a 9 day absence, and made a great effort to reach her. Her initial quiet contentment was followed by excitement and vocal expressions of pleasure.

**2;0**  The speed with which the child's ability to recognize expanded during the next time period can be seen from her behavior when she, because of a trip to Berlin, was away from Breslau for 5 weeks. The absence was almost as long as one that had occurred 6 months earlier during a summer trip. But instead of the "gradual dawning" that we had observed previously, in this instance we found the child entirely familiar with and accepting of our Breslau routines. In Berlin, thoughts about Breslau had so retreated to the background that they were never mentioned, and they seemed to have become submerged entirely. But that was not the case, as the child required only the most limited prompting for those recollections to return again a full strength. The following excerpts, taken from diary entries we made at the time, will serve to elaborate this point:

"When on the morning after returning home father took Hilde out of her bed, she caught sight of her play dog and the doll on the shelf, and greeted both toys happily and with familiarity, saying, '*Wauwau lala*.' From mother's bed, she saw, lying off to the side, a large charcoal sketch on which there was, among other things, a figure of a horse, and she called out 'Brr Brr.' Had the picture not already been familiar to her, she would not have been able to recognize it in its position at the time, lying off to the side and in the poor lighting. When Hilde had been dressed, she did something very interesting. Before the trip, it was her custom that, immediately after being dressed, she would go to a drawer that contained her playthings. She would ask that the drawer be opened, and would then empty it, carrying its contents piece by piece to the low-set window sill across the room. In Berlin there was nothing comparable to this. When we first returned to Breslau, she ran around the room aimlessly without knowing what to do. Finally, mother opened the drawer for her, and that set off the pleasure of finding her things again. With the first item in her hand, her body seemed to rediscover the way to the window sill, and the rummaging began anew in the old way after an interruption of 5 weeks. Gleefully she greeted and named every item, the '*wabba, wabba*' (rabbit), '*baaa, baaa*' (sheep), '*rrr*' (toy coffee grinder), and so forth; and as this activity jogged her memory, her recognition of the entire apartment followed naturally. Showing no sign of surprise, Hilde ran into the dining room and the study, into the kitchen and the corridor, everything as familiar to her as if she had never been away. In Berlin, Breslau had been forgotten and conditions there (in Berlin) were to her what was normal; here the situation is reversed back again."

**2;0**   The separation of the child from her nanny, which overlapped partly with the previously mentioned trip to Berlin, had been even longer, 9 weeks. Several times during the first 4 weeks we showed Hilde the picture of the nanny, whom she identified by name, but we did not do this again during the last 5 weeks of their separation. On returning and seeing the nanny again, our diary entry reads as follows: To the question: "Who is that?" Hilde at first gave no answer at all, or said "*oh no.*" By this she meant that she did not want to be bothered by being quizzed. But when we showed her the picture again, she immediately and correctly answered "*Berta*" and then also properly called the nanny by that name. Berta had not become completely strange to her. After this initial prompting Hilde named Berta often again and reaccustomed herself again to being with Berta, even if she also suddenly expressed some longing for the person who had looked after her in Berlin, and for her mother, and for the cook.

**2;6**   A further step in her awareness of recognition was established on returning from the next trip, during which the $2\frac{1}{2}$-year-old child had been away from the house for 4 weeks. On this occasion Hilde did not simply accept the old patterns as a matter of course, but consciously set out to reacquaint herself with things that had been submerged for so long. "When she climbed out of the carriage in front of our house, she vigorously stamped her feet with pleasure, saying '*House, house.*' On entering our home, she ran through the rooms with no hesitation, in happy awe, recognizing everything. '*Pretty changing table, pretty window, Hilde's closet*' and such things were continuously observed." On the playground, Hilde recognized, among others, a playmate whom she had not seen for at least 7 weeks, and quietly, shyly said his name when asked.

But around this same time, Hilde's ability to recognize made great progress in yet another direction: The latency that she is now able to overcome expands rapidly. We give just a few examples from our ever-expanding store of observational material.

**2;3** The 2½-year-old child recognized her grandmother without hesitation, whom she had not seen for 3 months. Hilde acted completely at ease with her grandmother.[3]

**2;4½** One and one half months later, Hilde again saw an Aunt W.— the latency time [since the previous encounter] was in this instance 4½ months. Hilde probably did not recognize her again immediately, but there must have been strong effects from previous encounters operating unconsciously, because after only a few minutes the child had regained her sense of familiarity with the aunt.

**2;9** The 2¾-year-old child recognized her grandmother again after a 5-month separation. At first view, Hilde hesitated a bit, then she made a movement as if to indicate that she wanted to run to grandmother in pleasure, but again stood still shyly. To our question, "Who is that?" she answered after a moment's thought, "*Grandma,*" although prior to her grandmother's arrival Hilde had not been told that her grandmother would be coming. Of course, in the time since her last visit, grandmother has been mentioned often, and Hilde has been shown a picture of her.

**3;1** The 3-year-old child recognized the previously mentioned aunt, in whose presence she had not been for 7 months.

**4;1** As a final observation, we note a recognition over a latency interval of 1 year. On her first stop in Jannowitz (on the religious observance of Pentecost, 1903), the child had had a continuing view of a large shed in the garden. On occasion she had entered the shed to look on as the laundry was being wrung. When on Pentecost of 1904 she again came through the garden, she ran right away toward the shed and called, "*This is where the laundry is wrung.*" This she did before she could have confirmed that the wringer was inside the shed.

# 2

# THE CHRONOLOGICAL
# DEVELOPMENT OF RECALL AND
# TESTIMONIAL ABILITY

For the concept of recognition, the sensory presence of the object of memory is still required. However, there is no presumption of a conscious projection of thought into the past. In contrast, recall in the strict sense is free of the sensory present. It reproduces the past impression as an independent mental production and—at least in its developed form— projects present thought into the past. It is a long developmental course from mere reproductions still lacking consciousness of past to a memory with a clearly fixed temporal position. We will give examples of the various phases of this developmental course to the extent that they are necessary for understanding particular memory functions.

In the further interest of orientation through the following chronological presentation, we discuss some aspects of psychological development that affect the development of recollection in various ways. Relevant here are (a) the content of the perception that is registered, (b) the circumstances that then reactivate that content, and (c) the time interval between registration and reactivation (latency).

With regard to the content of perception and recollection, a distinction must be drawn between momentary and continuous contents. The former include impressions of living spaces, persons in the environment—

in short, the entire milieu. The latter include experiences that stand out from the ordinary.

Further, the overall intellectual development of the child corresponds to a partitioning of the contents of recollection according to logical categories. Elsewhere, studies of school children have established a succession of three phases, which appear as *substance*, *action*, and *attributes*.[4] These phases can also be confirmed in the development of recollection in the small child. In the first phase, only substantial objects are items of recollection. In the second phase, activities of the child or of others appear. In the third phase, relationships and attributes are added.

With regard to the prompting of recollection, there is a major distinction to be drawn between a recollection that is in the broadest sense "spontaneous"—that is, issuing directly from the psychological activity of the child—or "provoked"—that is, prompted by others through questioning. Both forms appear simultaneously. Within that which we have just called *spontaneous*, there are admittedly various internal prompts. The most primitive of these is pure association: A chance perception leads to recollective images associated with prior impressions. "Freely occurring" recollections form the contrast to this, though admittedly the existence among children of this second kind of recollection cannot be proven conclusively. All that exists for an external observer of a child are the latter's recollective performances. The recollections themselves act like sudden unmediated "impressions" for which the internal associative link is not outwardly discernable. The higher stages of recollection are characterized by the fact that the will plays a role. In the case of perception, the will is involved in the initial "noticing of something." In the case of recollection per se, it is the mental recurrence that is brought about by the will (the "bringing to mind" of something). These higher forms of recollection appear relatively late.

The latency interval, which grows markedly with age, shows how the child, who at first lives almost entirely in the present, steadily develops into a temporally extended being, so that the temporal sphere of the I and its world is extended both forward in expectation, hope, and fear, as well as backward in recollection. Psychologically, it is noteworthy in this context that the extension backward (into the past) occurs later than does the extension forward. Although the future that has not yet been experienced is less real than the past that has already been lived, the former has much more significance for the child's psyche than does the latter. At a time when the child still cannot report on something that has just happened, the immediate future is already an object of expression. As an intentional being, the child wants something much sooner than it confirms something. But the future is an object of will, the past nothing more than a matter that is done with. This is documented in, among other places, speech phenomena, in such a way that the infinitive form of the verb is used in a futuristic sense (*essen* = I want to eat.) long before the first past participle occurs. Likewise, the temporal adverbs of the future—*then, tomorrow,* and so forth—occur much earlier than those of the past—*yesterday, a moment ago, previously.*

We return now to chronological presentation, which in this part is essentially concerned with correct recollection.

**1;7** The first mentioned recollection, a "freely occurring" one, was shown by the child at the age of 1 yr. 7 months. For 5 days, we had had a friend (Anna) as a guest, and she used the room next to Hilde's. Early in the mornings, she conversed with Hilde through the door while the two were lying in their respective beds. Two days after the guest had departed, Hilde called out from her bed early in the morning "*Anna!*" and asked mother: "*Where is Anna?*" With that she glanced at the door of the room where Anna had been staying.

**1;9** The following recollections have to do with isolated experiences: One afternoon when she was 1 year and 9 months old, Hilde received a doll as a gift from a woman she did not know. The child received the doll with pleasure. The next morning, mother asked the child, who in the meantime had neither seen nor heard anything about the doll, "What did the lady bring you yesterday?" Answer: "Doll."

**1;9** Christmas occurred at this same age. The morning after Christmas Eve, which Hilde had greatly enjoyed, she began to say, entirely on her own as father took her from her bed, "*Mama, gagack, lala, wauwau.*" (We had given her as presents, among other things, a duck (gagack), a piano (lala), and a dog (wauwau).

**1;11** One day, when father was lying on the couch in the study, the nearly 2-year-old child was given the task of fetching father's slippers. The next day, about the same time, when she saw father lying down again for his afternoon rest, she suddenly began trotting around exuberantly, back and forth, saying "*Shoes, fetch shoes!*" (I'll fetch the shoes!) The recollection of what she had done the previous day was awakened in her by the same circumstances—this is a clear example of a recollection being prompted through an association.

**2;0** The regular *switching* of living quarters between Breslau and Berlin offered a series of noteworthy observations about recollections that the child had. Of interest to us first is a negative instance. Hilde accustomed herself very quickly to the strange surroundings in Berlin. But we have already noted that when she was in Berlin, she did not demonstrate in any way discernable to us that she had any recollections at all of the circumstances in Breslau. Back in Breslau, however, her behavior was somewhat different. Here, recollections of Berlin surfaced spontaneously, if only sporadically. For a while, words like "*Omama*" (grandma), *Aunt W . . . Uncle E . . .* appeared in her speech. Many of these occurred several days after the return to Breslau. Coming back inside from a walk, she once expected to see "*Gettud*" (Gertrude), a maid in Berlin, instead of our Breslau maid, and things such as this. This variability of behavior seems to show that it is not the frequency and duration of an impression but its unusualness that enhances its retention for recollection. The 2-year stay in the quarters in Breslau had a more limited effect on the spontaneity of recollection than did the 5 weeks of events in Berlin. With our child we have repeatedly observed this both during and after all subsequent trips.

Beyond this, there is another notable psychological regularity worth mentioning, which showed itself in the first weeks subsequent to the stay in Berlin: The conflict between the present situation in Breslau and her recollections of Berlin embarrasses her. We noted this in this connection: "When we asked Hilde about the people in Berlin, she became obstinate and defensive. The vagueness of her recollections apparently disturbed her. She could not come to terms with the puzzling contradiction of here and there, now and then. Several times, when we asked 'Where is grandmother?' or 'Where is Aunt W . . . ?' we got impatient answers like '*oh no!*' or '*no!*'"

Around this same time, recollection begins to move beyond its relatively impoverished early stages and to play a constant role in the life of the child. Of course, the time frame over which recollection extends is still quite short, but for that reason frequency (of exposure to things) is very significant. Especially well-recalled are impressions of things that have been experienced a few hours previously or on the day before—for example, receiving gifts of toys, child games, a visit to the zoo, and other such things.

2;0  Here is one of many examples of this: "During a walk, Hilde saw roosters and imitated their crowing with a sound something like '*kikiki*.' On the following morning she began to crow happily '*kikiki*' and then came running to mother saying, '*Mama kikiki*.' Here had surfaced a memory of something that had happened the previous day."

2;0  A significant advance is suggested by another observation that we made of the 2-year-old child. The recollection did not remain isolated as a mental image of something past, but was instead used to draw logical consequences for something in the present. Admittedly, we are talking of a time interval of only a few hours. The child had let the ball roll under the hutch, and had tried without success to get it back, so the ball remained where it was. Two hours later, when father and daughter were playing a hiding game and father looked under the bed, Hilde was reminded again of the ball having rolled under the hutch, and she pointed father to the right place, saying "*The ball is lying over there.*" So along with the positive recollection that the ball had rolled away, she also had the negative recollection that it still had not been retrieved, and concluded that the ball was still lying under the hutch, where it had been left.

Gradually, the effective latency times are also becoming longer.

**2;1** When the child was 2 years and 1 month old, we parents took an 8-day trip away from home. We had an intelligent nanny, and she was directed to write down immediately every single expression by the child that related to our being away and to send her written observations to us. Here we quote our diary: "Hilde said goodbye to us downstairs at the carriage, of course not understanding that we intended to be away from her for an extended period of time. When we stood up in the carriage, father accidentally dropped a bottle, which fell out of its holder and smashed on the stones in the street. We did not notice that Hilde took special note of this. The following recollections became associated with this entire sequence. When, still on the same day, Hilde came back from her walk and did not find mother there, she said, '*Mama bye-bye with horsie.*' On the next morning, when Hilde went with the nanny through our bedroom, Hilde missed mother and said, '*Mama went bye-bye.*' But it was 5 days after our departure that Hilde made the most interesting expression of recollection. Though the nanny assured us that in the meantime no one had spoken about the matter, nor had anyone reminded the child of her parents, she suddenly blurted out, '*Papa horsey, bottle boke.*' (= Papa, horses, the bottle fell and broke.)"

**2;4** A quarter of a year later, the latency time potential has already tripled. When Hilde was asked about her sick nanny, whom she had not seen for the entire day, with the words "*Where is B . . . ?*" she answered, "*Was mountains*" (= She was in the mountains); "*Papa too, yes?*" The answer shows something noteworthy: Hilde says nothing about B.'s current whereabouts, but instead remembers that 3 days previously B. had been in the mountains. For the first time, she makes a reference to the past (uses the imperfect) with clear reference to something that is already some distance in the past. So too did it occur to Hilde in the same context that father had spent time in the mountains. It is virtually out of the question that this fact, referring to something that happened fully 2 weeks previously, had been mentioned in her presence.

Something completely lacking in the child up to now is the ability to temporally differentiate and to fix isolated memoric thoughts. The child is satisfied simply to recall something as having happened at some time in the past that is not further specified. Also, the child's perspective on the past is rigid rather than nuanced.[5] This is revealed, for example, in the context of lasting impressions that, with but small variations are part of day to day life: Walks, meal times, games, and so forth. The strong associations quickly made in these activities are projected in an undifferentiated fashion backward into an indeterminate past, and the child seldom has the occasion to express anything spontaneously in reference to them. But if by means of a question one presses for such testimony, the game of association is played out like a wound-up clock, because the higher stage of recollection, the "making one's self aware," is still lacking—and the possibility for falsification emerges. So just as it is true among older children that the way in which they are questioned is the major source of their false testimonials concerning what they recall, so is it also the case in early childhood that the very putting of questions is the first source of false assertions. We had occasion to note examples of this at the beginning of the 3rd year of life:

2;1 "Up to now there were some questions for which Hilde would habitually give a standard sequence of answers, whether or not they agreed with the particular event in question, provided that after each word one invited her to say more simply by uttering a questioning 'and?' For example, 'With whom did you go walking today?' '*Mama.*' 'And?' '*Betta.*' (= Bertha, the nanny.) 'And?' '*Papa.*' Or, 'What did you eat today?' '*Soup.*' 'And?' '*Meat.*' 'And?' '*Potato.*' 'And?' '*Pot.*' (= fruit compote.)"

2;3 Here we noticed the beginning of a change in the 2¼-year-old child: When questioned, Hilde began to distinguish between her impressions of the recent past. First example: "What did you eat today?" "*Soup.*" "And?" "*Meat.*" "And?" "*Pot—no.*" She corrects her mechanical listing: Specific memory prevails over the habitual association.

Second example: Yesterday after returning from our walk, we asked her about her playmates: "Did you see Fritz?" Answer: "*No, not today.*" "Did you see him yesterday?" "*Yes.*" Both answers were correct, albeit the second only coincidentally.[6]

From the next half year we select two accounts of recollections about experiences that are noteworthy because they involve a month-long latency period:

2;6 Once while we were spending time in the country, the child watched very attentively and tried to imitate us as we threw stones into a pond. After 1 month—H. had in the meantime seen no water—as we went walking in Breslau and suddenly stepped onto a bridge, her first words on seeing the water were, "*Throw stones again.*"

If this recollection was the result of association, the next one was, as best we can judge, spontaneous. The child said suddenly, while in the midst of a game: "*Aunt E. . . .*" Mrs. E, a woman who was previously completely unknown to the child, had visited us no less than 4 weeks previously. In the interim, Hilde had perhaps heard the woman's name uttered once in conversation. To test if Hilde's mentioning of the woman's name was linked to a recollection of the woman herself and of the situation in which Hilde had encountered her, mother asked Hilde: "In which room was Aunt E., then?" Answer: "*In the salon*" (a room used only rarely for visiting, but in which, in fact, H. had greeted Mrs. E.).

If before going further we consider the phenomena of recollection described thus far from the standpoint of the "stages of learning" mentioned at the beginning of this section, one sees in fact the chronological stage sequence: *substance, action, relations,* and *attributes*—not, of course, in such a way that the logical capabilities that come later replace these earlier ones, but rather that those logical capabilities take their place in the sequence formed by the other, earlier capabilities, and thus expand the domain of possibilities regarding recollection. Thus is the first half of the second year of life characterized by simple recognition, which obviously can be directed only to physically substantial objects. The first recollections of the next quarter-year relate to persons, and are thus also recollections of substantive entities. Among 21-month-old children the "action state" begins with recollections of specific happenings. And to the extent that, after a short while, H. also includes spatial aspects of the situation in her recollections and testimony, we see emerging the third and final stage, which incorporates "relations and characteristics." When she localizes the aunt in the parlor and the broken bottle alongside the horse, we have clear evidence of spatial relations.

It is not until around the end of the third year, however, that the stage of "relations and characteristics" reaches its culmination. The following examples may help to illustrate this, in that the child reproduces not only isolated characteristics but **also** entire situations with the various interrelationships they contain.

Some recollections of attributes were associated with grandmother, who had come to visit in Breslau. "Once, when H. was slouching at the table, mother said, 'Look, sit up straight this way, like mama.' H. answers, '*Or like grandmother.*' (In fact, grandmother maintains a strikingly good posture.) We asked further: 'Where did grandmother always use to sit?' And H. pointed correctly to her usual place. A month had passed since grandmother left. On another occasion—by this time, grandmother had been gone for 2 months already—Hilde saw her mother in a matinée cap to which Hilde was not accustomed, and cried in amazement: '*What do you look like? Like grandmother! Did you get it from grandmother?*' Grandmother had worn a matinée cap when she was here that, although of a different color was, like this one, decorated with white lace and in its casual style was similar to the one worn by mother."

We must discuss more thoroughly situation-specific recollections, which we treat together in the interest of achieving a better overview, even though in doing so we interrupt the chronological course of our presentation.

**2;10** The following situational recollection incorporates an entire system of separate moments, which at the same time constitute the longest latency time by far that had been exhibited to that point. When H. was nearly 3 years old, we asked her: "Who cut your hair? Papa?" (She had had her last hair cut 2½ months previously.) H.: "*No, Uncle.*" (= the barber; "uncle" is what she calls all unfamiliar men.) "Where then? Here in this room?" H.: "*No, in other room.*" (We had been to the barber in his shop.) "Where did he sit Hilde down?" H.: "*In chair.*" "And what did he pick up?" H.: "*A scissors.*" "And?" H.: "*A cloak.*" (A covering was tied around her.) "Who went with you? Papa?" H.: "*No, Mama.*" Everything she said was correct. It is noteworthy the way in which the certainty of her recollections enabled her to withstand the three leading questions inviting false answers.

**3;2** A recollection by the 3-year, 2-month-old child is relevant as well. After we had spent 4 weeks in Jannowitz with Hilde, we discovered that the new surroundings had not extinguished the old impressions of Breslau. On the contrary, both places were clearly distinguished from one another in her mind. Still, during this entire time she expressed hardly any reminiscences about Breslau. Still in Jannowitz on the day we were set to return, we asked her about objects in our Breslau apartment, about her playground, and so forth, she indicated that everything was as present to her as ever in the "*other go home,*" as she said so appropriately. We asked, for example, "Where is the piano?" H.: "*In the study.*" "Where is the changing table?" H.: "*In the bedroom.*" "In Hilde's?" H.: "*No, in Mamas.*"

Some later situational recollections awakened our special interest through the fact that the reproduced content was illustrated through a peculiar topographical demonstration. Just as an adult tries to make difficult relations of place clear by means of sketches on a reduced scale, so too does the 3½-year-old child support what she is saying by physical demonstration, using hand gestures. From the numerous relevant observations we have of this, we record two.

**3;7** In a conversation about the long-past stay in Jannowitz the question arose: "Where was Papa's room?" H.: "*Here*" (she pointed to a place on the table, as if a floor plan of the apartment were lying there). Mother: "Then where did Aunt W . . . sleep?" H.: "*Upstairs, and once she wanted to sleep here*" (she pointed to another place on the table).

**4;2**  Six months later, she reported one afternoon after her morning walk: "*We sat with Marie right here* (she pointed to a place on the table), *and then we played in the tree* (she pointed to another place on the table), *and then we went this way* (she traced with her finger over a section of the table), *and then around this way and back to here* (tracing her finger throughout)."

These topographical recollections contain two psychologically note-worthy aspects. They show first how vivid the visualizations of the child must be. None of the demonstrations would have been possible at all unless H. had been able to clearly visualize for herself the entire spatial layout. Second, these observations show how little recollection has to do with absolute size. On the contrary, how basic is the tendency and the capability to project unvisualizable dimensions of size and distance into the framework of what is visually possible.[7]

Let us return now to our chronological report.

**3;0**  When Hilde was 3 years old we observed for the first time a kind of recollection that proceeds from the will to pay attention to something. H. was given an instruction, and even though this instruction would be carried out after only a short interval of time, its effect was nevertheless quite surprising. When she awoke in the morning, Hilde was in the habit of calling out so that someone would attend to her, and so that her parents, who were lying in the next room, would ring the bell to alert the nanny. Hilde had long since made a firm association between our signal of ringing the bell and the nanny's appearance. Now one night when we were putting her to bed, we told her that in the morning she could ring the bell herself when it was time for the nanny to come and dress her. (Hilde could easily reach the bell when she stood up in her bed, and the ringing itself was great fun for her.) What struck us in this instance was how well Hilde had attended to our instructions of the previous evening. On the next morning she rang the bell appropriately, and afterward said somewhat gibberishly: "*As soon as Marie came, I rang the bell.*" (She meant: When it was time for Marie to come, etc.) In her fourth year, the recollections improved mark-edly in detail, in spontaneity, and in the length of the latency intervals. With regard to the correctness of details, we noted the following of the $3\frac{1}{2}$-year-old child in Schreiberhau: "Often Hilde returns from the woods and relates her little experiences; and when we then ask the nanny about the reported details, they prove to be correct. Or when an unaesthetic word from time to time slips out of her mouth, which she could never have heard from her parents, and we ask her 'Who has said that to you?' she most often identifies the person correctly."

The temporal extension of recollection is shown in the fact that latency times extending several months, which heretofore occurred only rarely, are now frequent.

3;1  The 3-year and 1-month-old child remembers impressions from 5 months earlier. She watched as mother washed her upper body and asked, *"Does the milk come from there?"* Her little brother had stopped breast feeding 4½ months earlier, and at no time in the interim had H. observed nursing.

Two groups of experiences that have given rise to especially strong and lasting recollections were the most recent Christmas celebration and journeys.

3;6  Hilde recalled the previous Christmas celebration in [the following] October and at the beginning of [the following] December; the latency periods in these instances were thus 9 and 11 months, respectively. The one recollection was prompted by the view of a small Araukarie, a plant that has a shape similar to the Christmas tree. Although the Araukarie had been in our living room continuously, it suddenly caught the child's attention one day, and she cried, *"Oh, the Christmas tree! It burned up tomorrow"* (for a long time now, "tomorrow" (*morgen*) has been used to refer to any time in the past; clarity in reference to time was not achieved until the end of the 4th year).

3;8  The second recollection seems to go back about 11 months. While looking at a picture of Santa Claus in a book, we came to talk about the coming holiday, and mother asked Hilde: "Do you remember where the Christmas tree stood?" H. pointed correctly past the table to the window, with an assurance that testified to a genuine recollection.

Especially noteworthy about the travel recollections of this year is the fact that H. was able to keep separate in her recollections two stops made during the summer trips that occurred close together in time and were very similar. On both occasions, at Pentecost and in August, our travels led us into the mountainous region, once to Jannowitz and once to Schreiberhau. It might have been expected that Hilde would confuse the times and places of these trips, and in certain respects this confusion did arise. For the most part, however, the recollections were clearly separated from one another.

3;8  Example: In each place, the house was run by a woman with whom H. became friends. The woman in Jannowitz—Mrs. A.—was already 60 years old, whereas the woman in Schreiberhau—Mrs. R.—was in her early 40s. The end of the second trip was almost 3 months past, and the end of the first trip was 6 months past when, while looking at a picture book one day, Hilde referred to one of the women as Mrs. R. Father: "Where was she, then?" H.: *"In Schreiberhau and* (thinking) *who was in Jannowitz?"* (She apparently was not able to recall the woman's name.) Father: "Mrs A." H.: *"But she was old."* Father: "Mrs. R. wasn't?" H.: *"No, she was new* (i.e., young); *and Mrs. A. always wore a cap.*" (In fact, the woman always had her head covered.)

**3;6**   Some additional reports about our travels that we noted: Two months after we had visited the cabin in Josephine (a resort in the vicinity of Schreiberhau)—in the meantime we had returned home to Breslau— father playfully imagined with Hilde that they were back in Schreiberhau and talked about the cabin in Josephine: "There was a garden, and we all sat there with Aunt T. and Thea, and there were many more tables, and people were sitting there drinking coffee." At this point, H. says to Father: "*And you drank coffee too.*" Father: "And what did you do?" "*I didn't drink coffee, I ate some snacks.*" (Fully correct statements.) At this point Mother joined in, saying, "And do you remember what I bought you?" H.: "A *sausage*" (an inflatable toy sausage). "And what else?" She did not recall the little cow bell spontaneously. Not until she was reminded that it was something to hang around her neck did she gradually remember.

**3;9**   Our return from Schreiberhau was already 4 months past when the following incident occurred, involving a recollection of the trip home: Mother was aghast at the manner in which the nanny was holding Hilde's little brother on her arm as she stood near an open window, and mother moved quickly to correct that. At this, Hilde said that when she was on the train she was only allowed to look out of a closed window and not out of an open one—and then more recollections surfaced in connection with this one. She recounted how she had looked out of one window while father looked out of another, and asked where father had gone: "*Did you go into the work room on the train?*" In fact father had, during that trip, retreated into another compartment to escape the noise of the children and to read, and he had often nodded to Hilde through the window.

**3;11**   One day, when it was suggested that the two children be put into the bathtub together, Hilde was enthusiastic about the idea, saying that this had been done once in Schreiberhau. This one instance in which the children had shared a bath had happened about 6 months previously.

**3;11**   During a discussion about the origin of various things, we asked Hilde: "Where do the trees come from?" "*From the truck.*" Mother: "They grow out of the earth." H.: "*But once in Schreiberhau I saw trees on a big truck, a big tree.*" H.'s recollection was entirely correct. She appears to have brought to mind a very particular experience, and was not merely thinking of the oft-seen trucks loaded with trees. Specifically, we had once been amazed by a huge tree loaded onto a very long transport vehicle, and with Hilde we walked along the entire truck, chatting with her about all of the things that occur to one when talking about a fallen tree. This experience, which has not been revisited in discussion for 6 months, seems to have left a deep trace.

**4;1**  With the completion of the 4th year of life, the possible latency time had grown to a full year. This claim is based on the fact that the example concerning the laundry shed discussed on p. 8 entails not only an act of recognition but also a recollection: *"This is where the laundry gets wrung."*

This concludes the diary-style report on the development of Hilde's ability to recall. By way of a concise overview of the chronology just presented, we summarize the results in two tables. The first shows how the various aspects of Hilde's recall abilities appeared successively with increasing age; the second lays out the growth of latency times.

Table 1 needs no further explanation, because it merely presents in condensed form all of the phases that we have discussed at length in the text. Table 2 is set up so that one can compare three different aspects of psychological functioning to one another either chronologically, in terms of the growth of the temporal intervals over which recall extends, or synchronically, in terms of how these different aspects compare with one another. The three functions are *recognition, spontaneous recall,* and *testimony given in response to questions.*

The table shows, first, at a given age, the latency time is longest for recognition, middling for spontaneous recall, and shortest for prompted recall. Thus we see, for example, that the 3-year-old child can recognize a person seen 7 months previously, spontaneously recall an impression first experienced 5 months previously, and can recount, when asked, aspects of a situation that had been experienced $2\frac{1}{2}$ months previously.

Second, the findings summarized in Table 2 indicate that the development of this child's spontaneous recall abilities can be stated roughly as follows: In the second year, recall extends over days, in the third year over weeks, and in the fourth year over months.

For the next 4 years we give only samples from the further development of Hilde's achievements in the domain of recall. We elaborate only in those instances in which the additional material offer a new perspective on what has already been said.

We spoke on p. 17 of a visualization ability that Hilde has in the domain of shape–contour relations, and of her tendency to portray the spatial relations she perceives not linguistically but motorically. In this connection, we observed at age 4;5 a typical example that, in contrast to what was happening earlier, steadily increased in occurrence, with a latency time of at least $4\frac{1}{2}$ months.

**4;5**  Once, while playing in Schreiberhau, she said with no prompting at

## TABLE 1
### The Development of Recall Ability According to Its Major Phases

| Age reached | | Recall feat | Latency time |
|---|---|---|---|
| Years | Months | | |
| 1<br>to<br>1 | 0<br><br>3 | First recognitions spanning several weeks | 2 weeks<br>to<br>6 weeks |
| 1 | 7–9 | First spontaneous recall of persons | 2–3 days |
| 1 | 9 | First spontaneous recall of specific experiences | 1 day |
| 2 | 1–3 | Recognition spanning months | 2–3 months |
| 2 | 4–9 | Spontaneous recall of specific experiences over several weeks | 2–4 weeks |
| 2 | 10 | Spontaneous recall of features | 2 months |
| 2<br>to<br>3 | 10<br><br>0 | Recall of spatial relations (situations) | 1–<br>2½ Months |
| 3 | 0 | Recall of instructions | 1 day |
| 3 | 1 | Recognition spanning more than ½ year | 7 months |
| 3 | 6–9 | Spontaneous recall of specific experiences over more than ½ year | 9–11 Months |
| 4 | 1 | Spontaneous recall of specific experiences over 1 year | 1 year |

all: "*I know where Fritz L. lives*" (a friend in Breslau). When she was asked to tell where he lived, she hesitated at first, and then when asked again finally answered, "*No, I won't tell you, but I will lead you there.*" Apparently, Hilde could mentally picture the house, perhaps the street or neighborhood, without being able to name things (she still did not know the names of the streets). Indeed, her mental picture in this instance was so clear that she believed she could lead someone there.

A special kind of recall that occurs only rarely at this age, and with respect to which accuracy obviously cannot be determined, is that of dream recall. Children's reports about dreams are believable at all only when their occurrence is both unusual and spontaneous. Children who are regularly

TABLE 2
The Growth of Recall Intervals (Latency Times)

| Age completed | | Recognition | | Spontaneous recall | | Prompted recall | |
|---|---|---|---|---|---|---|---|
| Year | Month | Latency time | Object | Latency time | Object | Latency time | Object |
| 1 | 0 | | father | | | | |
| | 3 | 6 weeks | living quarters | | | | |
| | 6 | | | 2 days | aunt | | |
| | 9 | 9 weeks | nanny | 3 days | grandmother | 1 day | doll gift |
| 2 | 0 | | | 5 days | broken glass | | |
| | 1 | | | | | | |
| | 3 | 3 months | grandmother | 2 weeks | father's trip | | |
| | 4 | | | 4 weeks | throwing rocks into water | 3 days | nanny's trip |
| | 6 | | | | | | |
| | 9 | 5 months | grandmother | 2 months | grandmother's clothing | | |
| | 10 | | | | | | |
| 3 | 0 | 7 months | aunt | 5 months | brother's nursing | | |
| | 1 | | | 9 months | lit-up Christmas tree | 2½ months | haircut |
| | 6 | | | | | | |
| | 9 | | | | | | |
| 4 | 1 | 1 year | shed | 1 year | wringing of laundry | 11 months | placement of Christmas tree |

asked to "tell what you have dreamed about" gladly do so, because they are inclined to playful fantasies anyway. In our nursery, discussions of dreams do not play any great role, and precisely for this reason a spontaneous account once given by Hilde counts as a notable exception. She gave this report 4 weeks after the birth of her little sister and 8 days after mother had finished convalescing.

**4;9½** *"Today my dream was all about people: how Eva says 'ayhay,' and how Eva is so cute, and how Günther cries, and how he wants to take everything away from me, and how mother was still sick, and that I love mother and that I love father and that I go for a walk with Miss W. (the nanny)."*

The recall latency time of 1 full year, observed for the first time at the beginning of the 5th year, is subsequently reached more regularly, and is finally surpassed by a considerable amount.

**4;5** H. saw some cap pistols in a toy store in Schreiberhau and said, *"I want another one."* Mother asked if she didn't already have one; she answered, *"Yes, but it is broken."* Mother: "Where did you get it?" H.: *"In Breslau; did you think in Jannowitz?"* In fact Hilde had owned a cap pistol 1 year previously in Schreiberhau. In the meantime it had been long forgotten, and no one had spoken with her about the toy. This recollection, which was correct with respect to content and incorrect only with respect to location, stems from an event at least 1 year old.

**5;4½** Twelve months later we elicited a recollection that again showed a latency time of 1 year. We were talking about getting lost. We asked H. if she knew where she once had gotten lost. H.: *"Yes, in Schreiberhau."* And then came a surprising recollection: We asked about who brought her back to us in that instance. *"A woman."* "What did she have on?" *"A kind of bonnet like great-grandmother's."* "What did you say to her then?" *"What did I say? Me? Nothing at all. But a boy and a girl came, we haven't seen them often, but they knew where I live, and the woman brought me back. The boy had a striped jacket on, with white stripes."*

We adults are ourselves no longer sure about the bonnet or the striped jacket, but Hilde talked about this matter with such conviction, as if she had just experienced it. We know that everything else she said was correct. Moreover, she displayed in this instance a certain critical attitude in that she dismissed more focused questions about the names and clothing of the children, saying, *"I don't know."*

**5;5½** The shed in Jannowitz, which has already been mentioned several times (see pp. 8 and 20), surfaces repeatedly in the child's recollections. When her little brother saw a wooden hut in the Swinemünder forest and said, *"looks like in Schreiberhau,"* Hilde said, *"Oh, I know what he meant; he* means the little wooden house, you know, in Schreiberhau, where the wringer was inside." Mother: "Was that in Schreiberhau?" H.: "Oh, no, in . . . Jannowitz." Unexpected relationships, once noticed, seem to be recalled especially well. For example, the fact that the shed in Jannowitz, in which the child had probably expected to find cattle, housed a laundry wringer instead, had become engrained in Hilde's memory. Nearly 14 months had elapsed between the most recent stay in Jannowitz and this observation.

**6;0**  The timespan of recall becomes steadily greater. Once we were conversing with the 6-year-old child about the coats-of-arms of earlier times. When we wanted to describe a bow and arrow, she yelled, "*Oh, like you did for me once in Schreiberhau: you bent a stick of wood and bound it with cord and placed another stick on it and shot.*" The experience had taken place $1\frac{1}{2}$ years previously; in the meantime, however, but quite a long time ago, we had spoken of this event in passing. At that time, recollection came but haltingly, and this rendered all the more surprising the confidence and clarity of her account on this occasion.

**6;8½**  Hilde recounted a recollection with a latency time of more than $1\frac{3}{4}$ years, and this certainly without any refresher in the interim. We were discussing ants, and we told Hilde that many kinds do not have eyes, whereas others do. She said something like, "*And many animals, for example, flies, have a hundred eyes.*" Mother asked in amazement where Hilde had heard this. She said, "*Well, you told me that once when we were in the old apartment.*" Mother dimly recalled an instance when she and Hilde were sitting on the window seat watching a fly. It must have been at least $1\frac{1}{2}$ years earlier, because we had already lived that long in the new apartment when Hilde made this statement.

The $7\frac{1}{2}$-year-old child already has "memories of youth." A few experiences that lie more than half of her life in the past have become part of her permanent store of memories, admittedly only by virtue of the fact that they have been refreshed from time to time in the interim. But one has the distinct impression that these refreshers have solidified her picture of the original situation, and that the later recollections are not simply calling to mind her earlier recall-based accounts. This is especially apparent from the fact that in the later instances of thinking back, elements appear that had not been mentioned in the earlier instances.

**7;7**  The primary example is again an experience that happened in Schreiberhau. Hilde spotted a napkin ring that an aunt living elsewhere had given her as a gift more than 4 years previously. At just this time, this same aunt was visiting us. Hilde said something like the following to her: "*Oh, I still remember how you gave me the ring in Schreiberhau, and we also*

*bought cowbells.*" In answer to the question: "What did you do with them?"
she answered, "*We hopped around all over.*" The bells on the one hand and
the napkin ring on the other had on many occasions in the interim been,
separately, the objects of her reminiscence (see p. 19), but their connection
in this instance, and the addition of the recollection of hopping around,
apparently go back to the original experience.

# 3

## FALSE TESTIMONY:
## MISTAKEN RECOLLECTIONS,
## PSEUDO-LIES, AND LIES

False testimony can mean many different things, depending on its source and on whether or not one is conscious of the falseness. Completely unconscious false testimony stems either from an errant initial understanding or a mistaken recollection. Apart from these are testimonies that are false in varying degrees of consciousness and that can be harmless or deceitful, depending on their motivation.

We reserve for discussion in a subsequent monograph a treatment of incorrect understanding. The material in this chapter is based on our diary entries for Hilde. We consider first the matter of mistaken recollections, and then discuss the theme of pseudo-lies and lies.

### MISTAKEN RECOLLECTIONS

The collection of mistaken recollections we have registered for Hilde is relatively small. This is attributable in part to the psychological makeup of the child, but it also results partly from the tendency of the observers to emphasize the new positive achievements made by the child in a function that is just developing, such as recall, and to record the recognizable progress that is made. At a time in which correct recollections occur, if at all, only in isolated instances, and during which chaos otherwise rules as far as testimony is concerned, false yes's and no's hardly stand out as something unusual.

In addition, a very young child is seldom questioned, and her relatively rare spontaneous testimony is not as susceptible to errors as is testimony in response to questioning. Admittedly, this advantage of spontaneous testimony is grounded in a deficiency: In early childhood, freely given reports lack specificity with respect to time, a feature that is as significant for the value of the testimony as it is dangerous for the accuracy of the testimony.

Consciousness of time is one of those mental functions that is acquired with much difficulty and most slowly. The 4-year-old child still has a vague sense of the meaning of "long ago," and also can draw a rough distinction between "earlier" and "later"; but it is impossible for the child to specify an experience as having happened precisely "the day before yesterday" or "last week," to say nothing of tracing it back to a particular month. In the course of a day, a child can say, full of confidence, "thus and so was today," or "thus and so was not today," but hardly use "yesterday" as a way of specifying more proximately a recollection referring to something going back further.[8] None of this is contradicted by the claim that the child's recall spans objective time intervals extending far back into the past. What transpired a year previously certainly has effects, but the child has no conception of the timespan of a year. Insofar as the child is able to keep recollections temporally distinct from one another, he or she does this with the help of spatially grounded distinctions. Statements such as *"That was in Jannowitz," "That was in Schreiberhau," "That was in Berlin,"* are for the child not merely statements about locales but are also an imprecise way of fixing things temporally.

As already mentioned, it is by virtue of this deficiency that a major source of error in spontaneous recollections is eliminated. However, in the vast majority of instances in which questions about recollections are posed, just such a time-specification is demanded. One does not simply ask if the child has ever encountered playmate F. during a walk, but rather if that playmate was encountered today. The child is not asked if she has ever brushed her teeth, but rather if her teeth were brushed this morning, and so forth. But where such provocations are produced by harmless questions, one conjures up the image of a genuine Pied Piper calling forth a whole string of entirely innocent false recollections. The child says "yes" because the question in fact elicits the memoric image of the playmate or toothbrushing, and the exact meaning of "today" is still not grasped. And the question "when?" functions at best suggestively when it is understood at all, and is answered in a random fashion. So we have, as in many other cases to be discussed later, instances in which the question or interrogator is often enough the elicitor of false testimony.

**3;10** Now admittedly, not all of the child's mistaken recollections can be traced back to the source just discussed. On the contrary, many other causes of mistakes can be discovered. First, we give an example of how interest in a subject can have the power to falsify testimony on that subject. The mother's report of this instance runs as follows: "On a walk to the park during February, I spoke with Hilde about the swans living at the lake, and we were both very curious to find out if we would see them when we arrived there. But there were no swans, because a thin layer of ice still covered the pond. We talked a while longer, wondering if maybe the swans were hiding in the little swan-huts in the water, and what it might look like inside those swan huts. Then, on our way back, we talked about other things. As we walked along, I asked Hilde 'What will you tell Father?' She answered promptly, '*That we have seen swans.*' I: 'What did we see?' H.: '*Many swans.*' I: 'Did we really see swans?' H. (reflectively): '*No, they were inside the huts.*'" With what confidence had Hilde first claimed to have seen the swans! This shows that the content of something in which one's interest has been strongly stimulated can seem to have been actually experienced even in the absence of sense perception.

Another mistaken recollection at the same age shows how habitual associations can blur the effect of a one-time experience. The observation is analogous to experiences that otherwise often occur in studies employing pictures.

**3;10** We gave H. a black-and-white photograph portraying two eagles attacking a seagull over the water. H. looked at it briefly but with great interest, and mother explained the picture to her. About 2 hours later we questioned her on the contents of the picture, and H. recounted them correctly. A leading question designed to induce error was not successful. ("Weren't the eagles sitting on the ground?") In contrast, questions about the color of the sky and of the eagles were answered "*blue*" and "*brown,*" respectively. Even when repeatedly warned to "think about it some more," H. stuck with brown and blue.

No striking instance of mistaken recollection is noted again until age 6;0. There must have been many in the interim that for one reason or another escaped observation or recording.

**6;0** We were in the dining room talking about books, and in speaking of one book she asked if perhaps the man who had written it was the one whose bust was on the pedestal behind the piano. "*Oh yes, Goethe,*" it came to her all of a sudden. We asked incredulously, "Where is he standing?" Hilde: "*You know, behind the piano in the next room.*" In reality, the bust of Goethe to which she was referring was not in the next room with the piano, but instead in still another room, standing between two windows. In this case, we were dealing with a mistake that resulted from an amalgamation of impressions of our current home with those of the previous one that we had left 10 months previously. Here as there the dining room adjoins a room with a bay window where the piano stands in the same relative position. In the first apartment, the bust was in fact behind the piano, but in the new apartment the bust was placed in a third room from the time we moved in. Hilde maintained her claim so persistently that we sent her into the next room to check, and even there she did not detect her mistake immediately on looking at the piano but instead asked in amazement: "*Oh! But where is the pedestal? It is not there any more.*" Not until she was sent into the third room and saw the pedestal with the bust did her mistake become clear to her.

**6;0**   Shortly thereafter we noted a significant size confusion. At Easter, she had received a toy rabbit as a gift, which mother took for safe keeping. After 24 hours, mother returned it to Hilde. However, Hilde was firmly convinced that the rabbit returned to her was not hers. She thought that hers had been much larger, and she wanted to have her own. Mother had no other rabbit, and explained this to Hilde, but she really would not be convinced, and protested repeatedly that her rabbit had really been much larger. It may be that this mistake was in part a result of the fact that around Easter she often had the opportunity to look into the shop windows at large rabbits. Moreover, on the previous Easter she had been given a rabbit twice as large, which she vividly remembered, and her recollection of this other rabbit might now have melded with that of the new one.

**6;10**   When Hilde was 6;10, we used a sequence of picture puzzles to make a little study of testimony. These puzzles were contained in one of her picture books, and she had already seen them often without, to this point, being able to solve them. This time we explained to her the way to solve them, and she easily went right through the sequence. Afterward, we asked her about the color of the puzzle pictures. The results are shown in Table 3.

Almost half of the colors she gave were incorrect. These errors resulted partly from old associations as when the beds were said to be white, the basin white and blue, and the rockers of the rocking horse brown. Naturally, H. had not paid attention to the colors when she was solving the puzzles. Thus was confirmed a point made previously: The lack of attention in perception does not lead to impoverished testimony but rather to testimony that contains many errors.[9]

## TABLE 3
### Hilde's Answers to Questions About the Colors of Puzzle Pieces

| Questions | Answers | (Actual colors) |
|---|---|---|
| What color is/are | | |
| the sleeves? | *blue* | (green) |
| the cake? | *yellow* | (yellow) |
| the basin? | *white and bright blue* | (only blue) |
| the shoe? | *red* | (red) |
| the rocking horse? | *white* | (white with red spots) |
| the horse's tail? | *I don't know* | (bright blue) |
| the rockers? | *brown* | (green) |
| the bed? | *natural brown* | (brown) |
| the featherbed? | *white* | (green and blue) |
| the nest? | *blackish* | (brown–black) |

Additional experiments on testimony that we conducted with Hilde using pictures will be discussed later, in the comparative section.

## PSEUDO-LIES AND LIES

Lies are consciously false assertions made with the intention of deceiving others. Both features are required: If a speaker is unaware that what she or he is saying is false, then there is no lie. Moreover, if the speaker is aware that what she or he is saying is false but has no intention of deceiving, then again there is no lie.

Up to the moment of this writing—in other words, into Hilde's 9th year of life—we find nowhere in our observations of her a clear instance of lying in the sense just defined. The various objectives that would be served by conscious deception are—and up to now have been—entirely unknown to her.

When she was 4 years old, we wrote the following in a summary brief:

"H. never tries, through the instigation of false beliefs, to place the blame on others, or to escape a punishment, or to place herself in a more favorable light and others less favorably. Up to this age, she still has no idea that there is anything other than the most naive openness. Yes, and even more, she admits, without even being asked, every sort of little happening, misbehavior, etc. Thus, for example, she runs to father when he arrives home, and tells to him that she has so disturbed mother, or she comes to mother to admit that she has hit her little brother."

At this point, when Hilde is more than twice as old as she was at that time, we can only repeat this favorable report. (In stating this, we should note that H. receives home schooling, and is thus removed from the many-faceted sources of deception that most other children regularly encounter in school life.)

The following observations provide evidence of Hilde's continuing forthrightness from ages 4 to 8 years. These examples come from diary entries made by mother.

**5;11½** "Hilde had been alone in a room. Suddenly she appeared with a worried face at the threshold of the adjacent room and stood quietly before me. I: 'Hilde, what is it?' At first she gave no answer. Finally she began, '*I have cut my finger*' and, coming nearer, she shows the slight, barely visible injury. Yet she did not stop there. Hesitantly the words came from her lips: '*I didn't do anything in there the whole time. You know that, don't you. I just hurt my finger.*' I scolded her, but as mildly as possible."

Fifteen months later, still the same picture:

**7;2** "Today she misbehaved. I had long since forgiven her and kissed her goodnight when she called me back into her room: '*Tell Father.*' I (amazed): 'What?' '*That I misbehaved.*' Father had not been able to say goodnight to her because someone had come to visit; otherwise she would not have failed to tell Father herself in private."

These examples are merely chronicles of her customary behavior pattern. She is also quite concerned to let her tutor know if she has received even so much as a little assistance with her homework.

But if genuine lies are absent, there are nevertheless instances that would give the uncritical observer the false impression of lies. Psychological investigation shows that, for the early childhood years, a wide middle ground of *pseudo-lies* must be recognized. This ground lies between the unintentionally false assertions caused by self-deception (errors of perception and of recollection) on the one side and those assertions consciously intended to deceive another (genuine lies) on the other side. This territory is as plentiful in false interpretations by adults as in false assertions by children.

In this context, as in others, a distinction must be maintained between prompted and spontaneous testimonials. A prompted pseudo-lie occurs when the suggestive strength of the interrogator sets off an affective reaction such that the answer appears to be confirmatory. We ourselves have strived to avoid leading questions as much as possible, so as not to create in our child the anxiousness that is so regularly caused by penetrating questions. Virtually all of the pseudo-lies provoked by us (most of them unintentionally) could be traced back to affect-laden wishes. In this connection we have specifically gathered examples involving the answer fragments "*yes*" and "*no*." Both words can have a volitional as well as a declarative character, for they answer equally well the questions: "Do you want something?" and "Was that true?" Yet in accordance with the overall psychological condition of the child, it is the volitional character of these assertions that is not only primary but also the more resilient. Often enough, it remains a factor even when the question calls for a declarative answer. A pseudo-lie is the result. A couple of examples may illustrate this.

On the word "*no*" we noted the following in our diary entries:

**2;6** "'*No*' as defense against being reminded of something unpleasant.— The child of 2 years 4 months pinched her little brother after showing him some tenderness, so that the latter, while drinking, cried out loudly. Mother reprimanded H. Then, 2 months later, when mother later said, 'What did Hilde do to her brother? She hurt him!'—Hilde rejected this with the words '*no, no,*' obviously finding this scene unpleasant. Even her face showed how unpleasant she found this recollection. This '*no, no*' was not intended to signify that she did not hurt her brother, but rather to indicate a defensive wish: 'No, I don't want to hear about that,' just as in analogous cases the adult makes defensive movements.'"

Complementing this, we offer an example of a "*yes*" that appears to be declarative but is in fact volitional.

**3;0** "Today we were with H. on a scenic overlook, from where one could see far into the distance. We called H.'s attention to many things, saying 'look there at the tower, there at the smokestack where the smoke comes out.' H. always tried to fix her gaze on whatever we were pointing out. When we would ask her 'do you see?' she would always answer '*yes*,' but sometimes she would say '*yes*' when it was clear that she did not really see what was being pointed out. We tested her with a leading question about a flying bird that was not there at all, and the response was once again '*yes*.' At that we pressed her, saying, 'You don't see it at all; when you don't see something, you must say no.' Then, minding us carefully when we repeated the question, she said '*no*,' but immediately thereafter, on the very next occasion, she again said '*yes*.' This was no lie, for H. did not have the slightest interest in deceiving her parents. In her ambition and her desire to see, she simply would have been happy to have been able to see the bird or the rider or what have you. It was this very wish to have the experiences we intended for her that she was expressing by saying '*yes*.' It was not a declarative 'Yes, I see that,' but instead a wishful and expectant 'Yes, I would very much like to see that.'"

The prompted pseudo-lie is of an entirely different nature from its spontaneous counterpart, and it is this latter that plays a much greater role in early childhood. It is but one of the forms in which the child's continuously active play fantasy is expressed. Just as the child plays through activities, so too she or he plays through verbal expressions. In principle, there is no difference between pretending to be shopping at the moment, by going around the room, stopping at the door as if interacting with a merchant, asking for butter and eggs and saying "*thank you,*" and so forth, or, alternatively, dispensing with the actions altogether and resorting instead to portraying the events verbally, as having happened in the past. She might say, for example, "*I bought that.*"

We encounter the oft-drawn parallel between children's playful testimonials and poetry: The fantasy substitutes the possible for something that has really happened and gives the former the appearance of reality, without any purpose apart from the fantasy itself. What the child says is often only an expression of his or her momentary subjective imagination, whether this happens to match some objective past reality or not. Here are some examples from our diary that may serve to clarify this.

**3;5** "For a long time, H. has loved to tell stories as if she had experienced the events herself. The events in question are often rooted in something she has heard someone say, but in her fantasy they are revised and colorfully embellished. Naturally, we are not inclined to disturb or interrupt her creations. For example, H. once told mother something like the following while they were walking in Schreiberhau: "*I went with dolly to the new Silesian mountain cabin; there were cats on the top, a big cat and little kittens, the big one was black and the little ones were white . . . ,*" and so forth. (We parents have often gone off on excursions in the mountains, and H. has heard us speak of this. Cats, black and white, are something H. sees here almost every day. And the doll, as a trusty companion on her trips of fantasy, plays an important role in the stories she tells.)"

In general, most of the stories she makes up revolve around the doll theme, and this is no less true of her as a 4- to 5-year-old than it was when she was 2 to 3 years old. At times she tells us all manner of fabricated things, things that really could have happened but that, in fact, have not. Examples: "*Today I bought another new doll, she is taking off her blouse*" or "*I bought a little bed for the dolly.*" At times she attributes to her doll all manner of utterances, deeds, misbehaviors; gives the doll wishes that in her own experience have not been fulfilled. Also, she blames the doll for little transgressions of her own. Examples:

**3;2** Sometimes she makes up a word, and then attributes it to the doll, saying "*Dolly said . . . ,*" just so she can then laugh at the doll and say: "*That's just silly.*"

"*Dolly disturbed me so that I couldn't sleep.*"

One evening, H. called from her bed requesting a roll to eat, and then, when her request was denied, she said, "*Dolly wants one, too.*"

Once, when she was in the garden and warned not to tear off leaves, she answered, "*Dolly tore off the leaves; she gets a spanking.*"

The fact that these false statements are made in play is brought to light by the remarkable fact that deflections of blame from herself, as in the last example, Hilde has never put the blame onto real persons, such as her little brother or the nanny.

A striking example of the intensity with which Hilde relates her fantasies, and of the tenaciousness with which she maintains the appearance of reality is given by the following observation:

While looking through a picture book of animals, H. asked mother if this or that one could be petted—for her, that was the basis for determining the wildness or tameness of the animal. In the case of the raccoon, mother took poetic license and allowed that it could be petted. With that, H. began to tell a story: "*You know how I once was with dolly in the zoo? There we also petted the polar bears and the brown and black bears.*" Because on this occasion instructional lessons were being given, mother tried to bring H. back to reality, and said that one could not pet such animals because they are wild. In opposition to this, Hilde began tussling with mother, and in the exuberance of the struggle she scratched herself on a pin. Mother ran quickly for a bandage, and when she returned to H. she continued to cry over the pain as the bandage was applied. Yet despite this, she had to air what was in her heart, and with big tears in her eyes and a sobbing voice she cried out: "*But dolly and I did pet the brown bear and the polar bear!*" Comforting her, mother said with an understanding voice: "Yes, yes, you petted them."

Of course, exaggerations of such proportions did not occur every day, but there were countless variations of fantasies of this sort. We have given but a few examples. The entire life of our child was characterized by confabulations without harming her healthy ability to give objective accounts, or her objective sense of reality, or her ethical impartiality. It would be a complete distortion of the facts to characterize these as instances of lying, because when seriousness and play are still not separated in the life of the child, truth and lying cannot be separated either.

Hilde was not introduced to the concept and moral significance of lying until she was in her 5th year. Happily, this familiarity remained a purely theoretical one. We were continuously on the lookout for matters of relevance to this theme, and we have compiled the list of entries we eventually made. The results are as scanty as they are harmless. The notes extend only to the beginning of the 6th year; beyond this nothing more on this subject was recorded that is worthy of mention.

**4;4½** "When I go shopping with Hilde and she stands waiting for me in the shop where there are enticing things to eat, or when in the evening she is present while her parents are eating, she suddenly says: 'Oh, I'm *starving!*' In such instances she is not really hungry, but instead simply responding to the sudden desire to have for herself some of the 'goodies' that she now sees. She then makes use of this little verbal stratagem, which she has often seen used by her older playmates, to get herself a taste of something."

**4;7**  In contrast, the following case seems to be simply one of imprecision in the use of words. When the child is lying in bed and told that she should sleep, she often answers "*I am already sleeping.*" What she means is, "I'm already going to sleep." Once, when she was supposed to sleep at an unusual time of the day, she came wide awake to us in the next room after only a few minutes, and in response to our admonition "But you were supposed to sleep," she said "*Yes, I've already slept,*" which was clearly not the case. We would like to understand this to mean: "I have done my part; I have tried to sleep."

The relatively most serious instances of untruthfulness—but at that not matters to be taken all too seriously—were those that we observed in isolated instances around the same time. These had to do with attempts to put a positive face on questionable claims or behaviors, at which point serious objection sufficed to cause retraction. For example, she was once eating an apple that had been cut into pieces, and mother asked her if she wanted to give father a piece. What that, she broke off half of a small piece. Mother said in an admonishing way: "You're only going to give a half of a piece?" Hilde replied, excusing herself: "*I just wanted to break it.*" Mother: "But Hilde!" Hilde (still excusing herself): "*I wanted to give father first the one piece and then the other.*" The parents made it clear to her that what she had said was false, and she admitted it.

One sees from this example that the question initially prompts the attempted lie; it would not have occurred to the child on her own.

**5;1**  Similarly provoked, and perhaps from the very beginning not meant seriously, is the following instance: Hilde made a request of the nanny, to which the latter responded with the question: "Is it OK with your mother?" Hilde answered insolently: "*Yes.*" Nanny: "I'll ask her now myself." Hilde: "*Oh, I was just kidding.*" Hilde knew that it was not impermissible to say something false in play, but whether her "*yes*" was really meant playfully from the very beginning could not be determined in this instance.

The common thread running through the just mentioned examples of momentary untruthfulness is their self-centered nature. From time to time minor falsehoods also occurred that stemmed from altruistic motives and for this reason were even less serious. These cases usually involved protecting her little brother from being upset. Without doubt, her parents have served as examples in these matters. There are even instances in which a secret is involved, and the distance from secrecy to denial is not great. For the child, this gap is certainly below the moral difference threshold. Mother had offered cake to Hilde and to other children who had been invited as guests. However, she did this in such a way as to keep the matter secret from Günter, who could not have any because of an upset stomach. Similar tactics often occurred to Hilde, and she once did this in what turned out to be an unsatisfactory way:

**5;1**   "Once when they were out somewhere, Günter[10] gave her a leaf to carry, which gradually became a burden to her because it hindered her play. But Günter kept a close watch on her, so that she would not throw it away. But now, using signs, I tried to communicate to Hilde that she could drop it in a moment when he was not watching. Finally she threw it aside. But Günter noticed what she had done, and before I could intercede, H. tried to head off his easily aroused anger by saying to him in a calming voice *"Oh, it was only by accident, the wind blew it away."* But at this I intervened and made it clear to her that although she was permitted to throw the leaf away, she was not permitted to give any reason for having done so other than the true one."

# II

## COMPARATIVE PSYCHOLOGY OF TESTIMONY IN EARLY CHILDHOOD

We saw in part I how recollection and testimony develop in a single child. A comparative perspective must now be positioned alongside the individualizing point of view, so that the entire problem can be placed on a broader foundation and certain features generally characteristic of early childhood can be discerned.

Admittedly, the material on which we are depending is still not as extensive as one would wish. It is limited to children of the educated class, and in many sections based only on observations of our own children. As rich as the literature is on this problem with regard to children of school-age, it is quite meager with regard to the small child. Specifically, to date children ranging in age from 4 to 6 years have scarcely been considered at all.

Future inquiries will have to supplement the present investigation with observations of children of working-class status. This is an area in which public kindergartens will offer a valuable arena for scientific work.

# 4

## RECOGNITION

On the topic of recognition, we consider only those cases in the literature in which age and latency time have been explicitly mentioned. To the extent that those cases occur prior to the end of the first year of life, they provide a welcome addition to the examples on p. 5 from Hilde, where the first note is dated 1;0.

Admittedly, the reports on this earliest age must be judged very cautiously, and we will sometimes be required to place a large question mark after the recollective accomplishments we have portrayed.

### THE FIRST YEAR OF LIFE

0;5½ At the age of 0;5½, E. and G. Scupin's son [Scupin & Scupin, 1907, p. 19] showed no familiarity with his grandmother who had been gone 10 days. On the contrary: "The boy let out a terrible cry when he first looked at her and heard the sound of her voice, and also sat immobile in her arms for several minutes with his eyes wide open. Only then did he show familiarity with her appearance and his little face again assumed its customary satisfied expression." This sketch leads one to suspect that there was not a complete loss of memory. On the contrary, the cry and the wide-eyed stare lead one to conclude that the child had mixed feelings of familiarity and unfamiliarity. Such mixed feelings easily lead to expressions of fear, especially in early childhood. A short passage of time during which the boy was in his grandmother's presence was enough to relax the boy's feeling of strangeness and permit his feelings of familiarity to dominate again.

If in this case recognition was primarily visual, it was aural in the following case presented by Preyer [1905, p. 227], according to Baldwin.

0;6½   This case concerns a 6-month-old child and "his wet nurse, who had been with him uninterrupted for 5 months and then been away for 3 weeks. . . . On her return, the boy looked at her in a way that indicated that she was not a complete stranger, but still he gave no positive indication of recognition, even after she had spoken. But when she sang a familiar tune to the child, complete and demonstrative recognition ensued.[11]

From three quarters of a year on, one also observes prompt recognition after separations of several days. Thus, the Lindners's son (0;9) recognized his father after 4 days, the Lipmanns's son (0;11) recognized his father after 5 days [personal communication], and Strümpells's daughter (0;11) recognized her wet nurse after 6 days [Preyer, 1905, p. 227]. Following a separation of 14 days, Dyroffs's daughter (0;11½) [Dyroff, 1904, p. 51] behaved toward her mother just as she had before the separation.[12]

## SECOND YEAR OF LIFE

Regarding the second year of life, we first point to private correspondence from Mrs. Lipmann based on observations of her son.

1;3   "We were away for 46 days, and when we returned, Hans in fact did not give any positive sign of recognition. Yet neither were we strange to him, because he did not act toward us the way he acts toward strangers."

1;6½   "We were away for 26 days. On my return, I awakened Hans. He was so tired that he hardly saw me. Next morning, he came running after me as always, as if we had not been separated from one another."

1;10   "I was away for 47 days. I returned from my trip yesterday, and when I took him from the bed to greet him, he seemed to recognize me right away. His doll was lying next to him, and the doll also had to greet me right away."

Meanwhile, at this time recognition is no longer limited to persons alone, but extends to objects and to the accustomed spatial environment. There are various reports of the confidence and energetic pleasure with which children greet their home and playthings after a trip.

**1;2** At an age of only 1;2, Dyroffs' [Dyroff, 1904, p. 51] daughter displayed happy recognition after she had been away from her parents for 11 days.

**1;4** Our daughter Eva returned home after a 3½ week absence. "To be suddenly in her old rooms did not seem to disturb her at all. She adjusted quickly; her surroundings were immediately familiar to her and she felt comfortable."

**1;10** Our son Günter returned to Breslau from a 4-week stay in Berlin, where he did not really become accustomed to the surroundings. However, we noted, "The adjustment he made as he returned to his old familiar circumstances was quite remarkable. On entering the rooms of his home he recognized them immediately and he was full of happy excitement. The first thing he did was to pull open the drawer of his little table and pull out a catalog. He knew immediately which bed was his and which was Hilde's, where the little angel was and the picture of children playing ring-around-the-rosey (the latter of which had hung on the wall for at most 14 days prior to the trip). . . . " (One half year later (2;3¾), Günter easily recognized his home apartment after being away for 9 weeks.)

At age 1;10, Preyer's son [1905, p. 227] even showed recognition over a time interval of 11 weeks. "He showed animated pleasure at seeing his toys again."

Noteworthy in this context are the motoric reactions that, without missing a beat, follow the old stimuli that in the past had been repeated over and over but that had not been rehearsed in the meantime. Günter's path to the drawer of the child's table, Hilde's reaching for the picture above the changing table (p. 6), as well as her readjustment to the customary path from the toy drawer to the windowsill (p. 7). Noteworthy also is the fact that when we return from a trip, the children immediately feel at home in the old apartment.

In the cases mentioned thus far, pleasure has been an effective element of familiarity. The following case is one in which displeasure is a key element in recognition. Mrs. Lipmann writes,

**1;7½** "For some time, Hans had been drinking out of a silver cup. But one day he burned himself on the hot rim of the cup and wouldn't drink from it any more. After that, we gave him cocoa from a glass. About 60 days later, I again gave him the cup. He recognized it immediately and refused to drink from it. Only after great effort did I succeed in convincing him that the cup was not at all hot, but even then he took it to his mouth only hesitantly and cautiously."

# THE THIRD YEAR OF LIFE

In the third year of life, the latency time is extended still further. Now the child recognizes not only persons or objects that she or he has come to know through continuous or repeated encounters, but also those that are encountered only occasionally or even only once. Thus at 2;4, Scupin's son recognized "all relatives and acquaintances" after 6 weeks' absence. At 2;10, our daughter Eva recognized after a pause of almost 3 months the seamstress, the stenographer, and other persons whom she had only now and then encountered.

Doctors are recalled especially well as a result of the negative affective tone that accompanies their examinations.

2;0½   Mrs. Lipmann writes, "Today we were visited by the doctor who had examined Hans 9 days previously. At the sight of him, H. began to cry. He hid behind me and cried 'Scared'!" [personal communication].

2;4   Similarly, Mrs. Lange reports, "At the age of 2½, Gerhard contracted an infection from a mosquito bite, which required surgery. Afterward, the doctor did not visit for 4 weeks. When he returned after a trip to the Balkans, G. saw him climb out of his car and ran away crying and calling out: 'He no stitch-stitch.' "

2;6½   Likewise mediated by feelings of displeasure are recognitions of the Lange twins A. and St. in the following case: "At the age of 2;6 they were photographed. They did not like the ride up on the elevator; because when it was time to go back down, they balked at getting back in. After 14 days, we were supposed to pick up the proofs. But when the twins saw the elevator they both cried and they had to be forced to get back in" [personal communication].

As additional examples of recognitions after a few exposures, or even just one, we relate the following:

2;0   Major [1906, pp. 212–213] reports of his son: "His grandfather gave him a toy as a gift and spent the entire evening with him, showing him how to play with it. On account of its fragility, the toy was then put away. When it was returned to the child after an interval of 2 weeks, he said 'Dahaw' (his name for 'Grandpa')."

2;0   Outdoors in the summer, Günter greeted an arbour (Laube) that he had encountered 2½ months previously during a 1½ week long stay, calling out Paube. In the meantime there had been no talk at all of an arbour, nor had Günter himself used the word again.

**2;2½** The Scupins [Scupin & Scupin, 1907, p. 115] wrote of their son: "During our visit today to his grandparents' apartment, which the child has not visited for a year, he ran immediately to the cuckoo clock and said expectantly: 'Cuckoo.' He would not rest until the cuckoo clock opened up." The latency time given is most unusual. There is no case known to us in which such a young child has maintained an impression for such a long time without its having been refreshed in the interim. With our Hilde, we did not confirm recognition over a 1-year interval until she was 4 years old (p. 8). Moreover, among children between 2 and 3 years old recall failures have been explicitly mentioned concerning events that happen but once a year, specifically, for winter-time impressions of snow and of the Christmas tree.

**2;8½** Written of the same Scupin boy [Scupin & Scupin, 1907, p. 227] 6 months after the previously noted achievement: "Today, the boy saw snow for the first time in about 9 months. He pointed to it: '*What is that?*' We let him guess. He thought about it, then he said: '*Sand, the sand is white, eat the sand. . . .*'" So the word and concept of snow had been forgotten entirely. Further: "The child had no more recognition at all of the Christmas tree from the previous year. He looked at the tree from all sides, and touched the branches, but he gave no sign of recognition." It was with the same unfamiliarity that at age 2;11 our Eva walked in the snow and looked at the Christmas tree.

Considering the foregoing, it seems to us that in the case of the cuckoo clock, perhaps the child's impression had indeed been refreshed in the meantime, but this had been overlooked by the parents. Perhaps it was simply the case that the grandparents had spoken to the child about the cuckoo clock. (For about 1½ years to around the middle of the time interval in question, the boy even called his grandmother "*Huhu*"—cuckoo!)

## SUMMARY

On the basis of the available material, we suggest the following regarding the developmental course of recollection:

The first acts of recognition develop already in the first months of life. They are conveyed through the expressive movements of interest in the sight of familiar persons who are part of the child's permanent environment.

In the second 6 months the ability develops to recognize such persons even after a separation that lasts days or even a few weeks. The younger the child and the longer the latency period, the more difficult and hesitant is the recollection. In these instances one often observes an uneasy suspension between strangeness and familiarity.

In the second year, recognition of the persons in one's environment extends over intervals of more than a month in duration. The recognition of familiar objects from one's environment after several weeks of travel also begins around this time. With this, the correct motor reactions (orientation in previously familiar spaces, getting out the toys, etc.) also typically develop.

In the third year one begins to observe recognition of impressions that had been made on the child only rarely, or perhaps even only once, especially those that have been accompanied by some strong affect (e.g., recognition of doctors).

In the fourth year recognition is already so advanced that only achievements with extraordinarily long latency times draw attention. These may be as long as 6 months to an entire year.

# 5

## CORRECT RECOLLECTION

Recollection in early childhood is a function that, unlike speech, for example, is not necessarily directly observable to others. What we are actually able to observe in this domain are always either occasional expressions that are (sometimes) just coincidentally blurted out, or deliberate responses to promptings. A child might have countless recollections that are never made apparent. Thus one cannot specify absolutely the time of a child's first recollections, or their frequency, or the maximum latency time that can be bridged by the recollections. But absolutes are not as important as relations, and in this regard comparisons are possible, not only within a child across various ages but also across the recollective achievements of different children, in such a way as to provide insights into the psychological aspects and developmental course of this function.

### SECOND YEAR OF LIFE

There are no reports of genuine recollections during the first year of life. In the vast majority of children—as was the case with Hilde (see p. 10)—recollections begin to occur in the second year.

In many cases, "first recollections" are noted as extending over very short intervals of time (only fractions of an hour), something that is easy to understand from the overall mechanics of memory. The primary effects of an impression have still not faded out and the slightest provocation can suffice to bring the idea back over the threshold. We provide several examples.

Major [1906, p. 200] and Egger [1903, p. 15] reported nearly identical observations at the beginning of the second year. They correspond closely to a note that we made of Hilde (albeit not until age 2;0; bottom of p. 12).

In each case, the child of the observer had left a toy lying under a piece of furniture. One half hour later (15 minutes later in one of the cases) they were asked about the object, and both reacted by turning toward the correct piece of furniture and retrieving the object. Major emphasizes that this is the first case of recollection he had observed with his son.

**1;10**  Lindner's [Lindner, 1899, p. 489] son used the dialect word "*maah*" (goat) to tell his father, who was returning home, that the son had seen a goat (which in fact he had, half an hour earlier).

**1;11**  Eva Stern once accompanied her mother into the kitchen and, thus reminded by the setting, said to her mother, "*Aunt give Eva piece sooker.*" In fact, the cook Toni had given Eva a piece of sugar 15 minutes earlier.

Another group of recollections is apparently tied to the 24-hour cycle of the psychophysical functions. Impressions linked to certain times of day return in the form of recollection or, as the case may be, expectation, at about the same time each day, whether they be prompted by analogous situations or perhaps by similar bodily states (fatigue, hunger, etc.). The previously discussed instance of Hilde fetching the shoes [p. 11] is a case in point. Here are some additional examples:

**1;6**  Deville [1890–1891, vol. 24, p. 29] reports of his daughter, "She has a sequence of cataloged facts in memory, which she recalls each day at the same time and only at this time. She is hardly awake before she is requesting her bath. At 9 or 10 o'clock she requests her hat and talks about taking a walk. She asks for the basket that is taken along, and for the newspaper that we take with us in the basket. We are hardly finished with breakfast and she asks for the coffee pot to carry into the kitchen, and she does all of this without anything have been done to prompt her recollection."

**1;9**  Scupin's [Scupin & Scupin, 1907, p. 85] son: "Should mother forget to carry him to father's room to say goodnight, the son reminds her immediately to do so: 'Papa nite' (go to father to say goodnight) . . . Once he was allowed to sit between us on the sofa when we were having coffee, and since then he says promptly, confidently, and repeatedly when we sit down to breakfast: 'sofa sit.'"

But in the second year of life there are also recollections with considerably longer latency times. With regard to content they are different from those just mentioned in that they do not concern things that are experienced frequently and hence customarily, but instead relate to one-time or rare happenings that, as a result of their extraordinary nature, make a special impression on the child. With Hilde we had found that the latency times of such recollections during the age period from 1 to 2 years were at most several days [pp. 11–12]. We begin by giving some parallel examples to this.

**1;5**   Professor Feucht [1907, p. 93] reports on his boy Oswalt: "O. fell face first to the floor and hit his face in such a way as to cause his nose to swell up. Some days later, he demonstrated his recall of this by responding to a question about where he had fallen by pointing to the approximate location on the floor. When asked what had happened, he snapped his head forward to simulate the manner in which he had banged it."

**1;6½**   Major's boy was shown some photographs [1906, p. 210]. Four days later they came to mind without any obvious reason and without his having been reminded of them. Immediately he went to the shelf from where they had been fetched previously.

**1;9**   Deville's [1890–1891, vol. 24, p. 131] daughter told of what she had seen 2 days previously in the zoo:

> *a va da* (la girafe grande); (big giraffe.)
> *maman pin manger* (maman [a donné] pain à manger); (mama [gave] bread to eat)
> *té a* (chèvre a [voulu]) (The goat [wanted] . . .)
> *papo apapé* (chapeau attraper) (hat chew)

**1;10**   On two occasions within a short period of time, Günter Stern had fed swans, ducks, and fish during visits to a park. On the evening of the second of these occasions, he was asked, without any prior discussion: "What did you give the 'pipip' [swan or duck] today?" He promptly answered: "*piece*" (= little bits of food). Three days later he was asked, again without any prior discussion: "To whom did you give a little bit of food?" Günter: "*Ducks*." "And whom else?" "*Tish*" (= fish).

But these latency times of several days are not the maximal latency times that are achieved during the second year of life. Whether the absence of longer latency times in our observations of Hilde is simply a coincidental result of not having had the occasion to observe longer achievements or whether this indicates instead that her memory could not extend further into the past can no longer be determined. What is certain, on the other hand, are positive achievements of recollection among children younger than 2 years of age that span several weeks, and in certain instances an entire string of weeks. The material comes partly from our own observations and partly from the literature.

1;4½  Worthy of immediate mention are the first recollections of any kind that we observed in our son Günter. "A bright strip of light caused by gas lighting was showing on the wall of the room, and this reminded Günter of colorful reflections of light that we had often created by the movement of a glass prism (the last time we had done this was 4 weeks previously). He ran immediately to the place on the wall (a position not identical to the one where the light was currently showing) where he had always tried to catch the dancing lights, and he grabbed and scratched at the wall, expressing wishful tones."

1;11  But much more remarkable is a recollection of Günter's that we observed to have a latency time of not less than 2½ months. "He heard Hilde talking about a 'Tafel,' [an easel] and right way he pointed to our easel and said: '*bow-wow*.' There was no dog there at all. But 2½ months previously, his mother had drawn on it for the children large heads of a dog, a horse, and a cat, and Günter had taken particular delight in this. To determine if at that moment Günter was actually recollecting this earlier event, mother asked, 'And what else was on the easel?' Gunter: '*grgr*' (horse). We are certain that in the meantime no such figures had been drawn on the easel, because we had been traveling."

1;11  The following entry was made concerning our daughter Eva around the end of her second year: The children had played "shoemaker" several times: The three of them sat around in a circle and pounded with sticks on the soles and heels of their shoes. About 14 days later, Eva (for whom the game had been great fun) was in bed, and without any prompting at all started up: "*Play shoemaker, tap, tap.*"

1;7  Scupin's [1907, p. 77] son: "The extent of the child's memory is astounding. Fourteen days ago, the boy had watched as mother cooked bacon, and had called an onion that had been thrown into the pot '*ball*.'" Today bacon was again cooked in the same pot, and when the boy saw the pot, he called out excitedly: "*There Mama ball bah.*"

1;9  The Wertheimers' little girl, about whom Preyer [1905, p. 229] reports, saw a picture of a Christmas tree and said immediately, pointing to the place where more than 3 months previously a Christmas tree had stood: "*Bring here! Stand up! Light up!*"

**1;11** The very first psychologically oriented observer of childhood, Dietrich Tiedemann, reports a case [1787, p. 34] that is relevant concerning his son: "On the 20th of July he came to a place in the house where about 4 weeks previously he had been punished because he had made the place messy. Immediately and without prompting he said who had once made the room messy and received a spanking. Admittedly, the words the boy used were not completely correct, but still he spoke clearly enough to communicate his thoughts. So there were ideas about that time that had remained. On the other hand, when asked about something that happened only a few hours previously, he didn't remember any more, probably because the recollection was at the time still mediated through actual sensations and not through the inner course of thoughts."

## THE THIRD YEAR OF LIFE

For the purposes of making relevant observations, the third year is very fertile, because on the one hand instances of recollection on the child's part are still not so ordinary as to go unnoticed, and yet on the other hand language is normally sufficiently developed to enable adequate expression of recollections.

Important progress is reflected in the fact that reproductions are no longer isolated and unconnected but instead are connected to one another in larger complexes. Admittedly, the uninterrupted flow of recollections through which past life gains a certain order and clarity is still lacking. Of the two orienting factors of space and time, the second is still not sufficiently developed to be applicable. At this age the sense of time is still so rudimentary that it fails in the face of long time intervals.[13] In contrast, space becomes fairly early on a central feature of recollections. That is, recollections are correctly localized spatially much earlier than they are temporally.[14] Of course, and as we mentioned previously on p. 28, statements about location (specifically in reminiscences about trips) also contain some ideas concerning temporal sequence.

It may be that the spatial milieu is much more effective in prompting recollections because, in contrast to time, it can be revisited much more readily. Thus do we find that the first stage of localized recollections involves instances in which the renewal of spatial perceptions calls forth impressions gained of a previous experience in the same location. The example from Tiedemann given previously is relevant. In addition, we noted in the case of our son Günter three recollections, all of which were prompted by the topographical constellation.

**2;1** We came to a harvested field that a few days earlier mother had hopped across to reach the children who were waiting on the other side.

On viewing this field now, Günter stood still and said: "*Mother hop hop*." Likewise he stopped at a little garden at precisely the place where some days previously he had seen a cat, and said in a questioning voice as he looked around: "*meeow?—not there*" (the kitty isn't there).

**2;1** When we went into the country to a place where we had stayed 2½ months previously, he asked at the sight of the garden and yard about the "*bu*" (Kuh = cow). On our first visit, the cows in the stall had awakened in him an anxious curiosity and he pulled us right to the correct stall. This was clearly a topographical recollection."

**3;0** Scupin reports much the same of his nearly 3-year-old son. They were passing by a house where, 8 days previously, they had heard the cries of a child and a scolding woman's voice coming from the cellar. The boy suddenly stood still and asked: "*Where is the bad child?*"

**2;6½** Correct recollections of location can surface even when the spatial location is not again visible at the moment. We have already noted this in the case of Hilde (p. 15). Another example is provided by Major [1906, 214]. During a 6-week summer trip his son had not had occasion to look at some color cards which his father previously had often used to conduct recall experiments with him. After returning home the father showed the cards to the boy again, asking the boy where he had usually seen them. He answered immediately: "*Papa's room.*"

Impressions gained on trips are especially potent seeds of memories. Even in the 2- to 3-year-old child, all the new experiences: forest and field, mountain and water, plants and animals, boat rides and farmland, and so forth, leave behind deep traces of such a kind that the past can still be relived full of fondness and pleasure after weeks and months. At times these recollections surface quite spontaneously. In other cases nothing more than a small prompting, such as the picture of a landscape, an animal, a waving flag, a word in conversation, is needed to reveal the ease and vividness with which the impressions can be recalled. The relationship to location is almost always present, though admittedly in quite varying degrees of clarity. In one instance the name of a place will be given, and one cannot tell if it is connected to a vague overall impression of the visit or to specific recollection of a certain location. Thus, for example, it appears with our daughter Eva that the recollection "*Binz*" is represented by a picture of the beach. In another instance, such a specific location is explicitly named.

From age 2;1 to 2;3 our son Günter had been in Schreiberhau, where he had gathered an abundance of impressions. The first weeks after his return clearly bore the stamp of Schreiberhau, and the boy's fantasies in this regard seemed to enrich what he subsequently experienced. "More than anything, he recalled spontaneously the way in which the cows had been tended, with the characteristic cry of the herdsman *"beday beday"* and the call *"wild cow,"* as he called a cow that had mooed especially loudly. In addition, one of his daily games was *"puff puff,"* recalling his train ride. Three and a half weeks after his return we attempted to determine through questioning whether or not specific recollections were present. We asked him about the dog owned by our hosts, about the village children with whom our children had played, about the inhabitants of the stalls, and in his immature language he was able to say something about all of these matters. Among other things, the children had played a game that involved sticking so-called wooden apples onto sticks and then flinging them far. In all likelihood there had been no further discussion of this game in the meantime. When we now asked, "With what did you throw the apples?" he answered promptly, *"stick."* We then asked him: "What was in the stall at L.'s?" First he gave the answer: *"Cows."* We: "What else?" Günter: *"Calfie,"* and immediately it occurred to him: *"Pet pet, Tina hold"* (meaning: I petted it, Christine held me while I did this).

**2;4** Soon afterward another recollection from Schreiberhau was awakened that had been latent for at least 1 month. The picture of a snake that had formed two rings prompted the words *"gasses, gasses"* (eyeglasses)—*Ella.* We: "Where does one put them?" G.: *"Eyes."* Explanation: While playing doctor in Schreiberhau, mother had made eyeglasses for the children out of cardboard and put them on, and a playmate named Ella had brought her own such glasses along. The double-ring formed by the snake in the picture reminded the boy of the eyeglasses, which in turn reminded him of having played with Ella.

**2;6** At the age of 2;6, this same Ella appears again. At this time, Günter had been back home from Schreiberhau for 3 months. A little picture of a child brought to his mind the girl, and immediately other recollections followed concerning the girl's activity with the cows: *"Whip, ay cows ay Ella; eat ay cows"* (the cows ate).

**2;11½** These reminiscences even extend into the next summer. Mother and child were looking at a book about plants. While looking at a bunch of blueberries (depicted large and colorfully) he said immediately: *"Saw in Schreiberhau."* In Schreiberhau, we had often brought the children entire sections of blueberry bushes, from which the children then picked off the berries. As a 2-year-old, Günter himself had still not picked any berries. This utterance is thus even more interesting for the fact that single berries of the sort that he was now seeing and eating in a large quantity had never prompted this recollection. He also said, *"Saw in Schreiberhau,"* in response to a picture of a particular kind of poisonous mushroom. He was not able to remember the name of the mushroom (*Fliegenpilz*), but the fact that we had often called the children's attention to this luminous poisonous mushroom has had a lasting effect.

With Eva, our third child, the recollections of a trip we had made were rich and plentiful. It should be noted that in her case the trip occurred between the ages of 2;7 and 2;9 and in Günter's case the corresponding trip had taken place between the ages of 2;1 and 2;3.

**2;10½** This even occurred 6 weeks after we had left the seaside spa Binz—granted that during this interim there had been much discussion of the place. She had a piece of paper in front of her, and we asked her to read to us about Binz. Eva: "*There are steam ships there. The steam ship sails and blows its horn and bellows smoke. Here is Binz.*" "Where are the ships?" "*Ships swim. They go like this*" (she mimics the motion of the rudder with her finger). Even in the ensuing days she took great pleasure in regularly going over this treasure of recollections. At age 2;11 she reported quite accurately the fact that, along with her siblings and her father, she had traveled "alone" on the choo-choo train from Berlin to Breslau. Mommy had stayed behind with Grandmother. This trip had taken place 5½ weeks earlier. Likewise, on seeing a small wooden bucket that she had not seen for a long time, she recalled correctly that "*Mommy brought this from Born-holm.*"

**3;1** Even still at the beginning of the 4th year, when the [aforementioned] stay at the spa was 4 months past, recollections of Binz surfaced that might well be mentioned in the light of their relevance in the present context. The sight of flags awakened in her the recollection of flags that our children had been given as gifts on the beach. The sight of an uncle who attended them at their bath prompted the recollection: "*When F. got into the tub with his bathing suit on.*" "Where was that?" "*Well, in Binz.*" "What color was uncle's bathing suit?" "*Black.*" Everything was correct, and it should be noted that in the interim there had surely been no discussion of the black bathing suit.

**3;1** The same holds for the following rather flexible reminiscence. While looking at a picturebook, Eva came across a beautiful picture of the woods. At that she became excited, and told a story along the following lines: "*Well, we were there once. We sat on the bench, and the sunrays came down through the trees. We ran down the mountain, and we ran among the benches.*" Mother asked where that had taken place, but Eva was not able to say. Still, there is no doubt that what Eva was saying was a clearly delineated recollection of an experience in Binz—specifically a stop that we made one afternoon in the "forest church," which consisted of many benches that had been placed among the trees. There we experienced a wonderful sunset. The fire-gold rays of sunlight streamed through the tree limbs. (The picture that prompted this recollection did not portray a sunset.)

Another large group of targets of recollection are persons whose pictures and names are sometimes linked with certain places, sometimes with particular patterns of behavior, and sometimes with both. Of course, a distinction must be drawn between persons who are regularly part of the child's environment and only occasionally absent, and persons who are only occasionally present. The following is a word-for-word diary entry that we made concerning our daughter Eva.

**2;2** "One morning, mother set off with Hilde for Graudenz. Looking out from the window, Eva had watched their departure in the horse-drawn buggy. Still 3 days later, hardly any spontaneous recollections had been uttered. On the first day, she did not call for either mother or Hilde, nor did she mention either's name while talking about something else. On the second day, as someone incidentally mentioned the word 'mother,' she said 'Gone with the choo-choo.' If she was asked 'Where is mother?' she would respond 'With the choo-choo,' or 'With the horse,' or 'Graudenz'; also "lin" (= Berlin). But that was all she had to say on the matter. In the afternoon of the third day she received apple juice at the table. Eva beamed, 'Well, I'm glad that mother has prepared this for me.' Not until we asked, astounded, "Mother?" did she puzzle over what she had said, and then corrected herself after a momentary pause: 'Else' (the nanny). Father: 'Why must Elsie do it?' Eva: 'With the horse.' It was indeed this laconically that she expressed the thought: Because mother is away on a trip. On the fourth day, she expressed herself spontaneously on this matter for the first time: 'Hilde bye-bye on choo-choo.'" When she was the same age, Hilde hardly missed her parents at all when they were traveling and spoke only rarely of the parents' absence (see p. 13). This shows the extent to which children of this age remain very focused on the present. Furthermore, they really do not understand the meaning of another "going away," and therefore have no lasting awareness of absence.

Just as in this case a certain activity awakened the recollection of mother, so it is the case that recollections of strangers are for the most part bound to ideations about particular activities. In one instance, 18 days after a seamstress had been working there, our daughter Eva began to say, quite spontaneously: "Miss Fischer is sewing in the playroom." It should be noted that when she spoke these words she (the seamstress) was not in the playroom. Six months later in Binz she recalled the seamstress, whom she had neither seen nor heard for at least 4 weeks. She grabbed one of mother's dresses and asked: "Did Miss Fischer sew that?" Another one of the child's recollections worth mentioning is related to a visit in Berlin. She was saying how she had once gone to Aunt P.'s home and Aunt P. played the piano, and there were chairs. This event had happened 3 months ago. At the time, they had played musical chairs.

**2;4**   Major's [1906, p. 213] son called out one day, entirely spontaneously: "*Maggie hut eah*" (M. cut ears). M. was a maid who 3 months earlier had been at the house only 1 week, and had often playfully threatened to cut off the boy's ears.

The examples given to this point show that at this early age the recollections relate almost exclusively to the visible. To be sure, much of what is heard and spoken is retained—as the learning of a language and the mastery of countless children's rhymes shows—but only when it has been impressed on the child through the summation of countless repetitions. In contrast, recollections of verbal expressions that have only been made once on specific occasions occur only rarely, and even then do not last long.

This normal forgetfulness on the part of the child for what is spoken, or for the content thereof, is pedagogically important. On the one hand, adults inappropriately exploit this shortcoming. For example, they promise to give the little one something later (to calm or divert the child) without intending to keep the promise. Now at times the child's forgetfulness will forgive this, but this is not so in all cases, and when the recollection unexpectedly surfaces and the child notices that the person in question does not intend to make good on the promise, this is a serious threat not only to the child's trustfulness but also to his or her own natural inclination toward trustworthiness. On the other hand, adults often do not consider sufficiently the forgetfulness of the child with respect to what is allowed and what is forbidden, especially when the matter in question is being dealt with for the first time. An order given once—for example, "You should not go onto the grass" or "Don't step in the puddle," and so forth —might at first be obeyed by a well-behaved child, only to be violated again a few minutes later out of pure forgetfulness.

In light of these considerations, it is not surprising that observers of children have recorded virtually nothing concerning recollections by 2- to 3-year-olds of conversations. However, we can relate one observation that we ourselves made of our daughter Eva.

**2;11½**   When she was just 3 years old, we had Eva photographed. To put her in a good mood, the photographer promised her: "Afterward I will show you our animals." But when the photography session was finished, he left without thinking about the promise he had made. But Eva did not forget. She energetically requested to see the animals, and settled down only when her wish was granted. The photograph was supposed to be a surprise for father, and so mother wanted to be sure that Eva would not give anything away. This was the first time that silence was requested of the child in a matter that she was still thinking about and which, under other circumstances, she would surely have reported to father when he came home. On this matter mother writes: "How shall I make it clear to Eva that she should not tell father about this? First I tried to impress on her: 'You should say nothing to father because it is supposed to be a surprise at Christmas.' Meanwhile I had the feeling that these words were not sufficiently understandable and would not have a lasting effect, so I found a formulation to which she reacted in such a way as to convince me that she fully understood. I said to her: 'You should not say anything to father about this yet; not until the tree is lit up should you say anything.' From time to time after that, when I would remind Eva 'not to say anything to father,' she would answer promptly: 'Oh, only when the tree is lit up,' and she behaved accordingly."

Still more striking is the child's following recollection, which likewise was related not to something visually perceived but instead to expressed thoughts—this time her own. During a conversation we were having one afternoon, she said laughing, "Hilde's not a lady." Mother: "Why not?" Eva: "Because she's not a stranger." Mother: "Am I a lady?" Eva: "No, you're mother." As other questions also showed, she would only consider women with whom she was not acquainted as ladies. Eventually, the correct meaning of the word must have been made clear to her, because $1\frac{3}{4}$ months later the following exchange occurred: She saw an article of clothing belonging to mother and said: "Like ladies have." Mother: "So am I a lady?" Eva: "Yes, you are already big; but once one afternoon I said that you were not a lady" (almost her own words exactly).


## THE FOURTH TO SIXTH YEARS OF LIFE

From the fourth year on, recollections are so common in the life of the child that only those that reveal something very special merit mention. As already indicated, we depend almost entirely on our own notes.

As achievements of memory, recollections with longer latency times are interesting not only in and of themselves, but also as testimony to the inner lives of children. Because even though children outwardly reveal their inner selves more than adults do, there is nevertheless much in the child that remains hidden from others but that nevertheless has left a lasting impression on the child and continues to exert its effects. Some coincidental event or other can reveal that an experience of the seemingly most indifferent sort has strongly embedded itself in the mind of the child, only to spring up again from the unconscious when something fitting occurs. The following recollections are all instructive in this vein, but especially so are two recollections by Günter concerning color. These stem from experiences from the beginning of the third year but do not surface for the first time until the fifth year.

What follows is a chronological report.

**3;2** Once in Swinemünde when mother was sick and lying in bed and the family was having lunch in her room, Günter said: "*Once in our old home when you were sick we ate in your bedroom.*" Mother: "Do you know where you sat?" Günter: "*Don't know, only the one thing* (= all I know is that we did that). The event to which he was referring was 9 months in the past.

**3;5½** The latency time for a recollection by Eva was not quite so long: "During the evening meal, recollections of Christmas suddenly surfaced. These were factually correct but temporally false in that Eva related them to a birthday about which she had just been speaking. The reminiscence proceeded as follows: "*On the birthday, you two sat on the bench; but Uncle F. didn't sit on the bench. And Günter* (laughing)—*oh he was Santa Claus, and he gave you (father) a cigar, and he gave one to Uncle F., too.*" The unusual situation in which both parents were sitting on the child's bench and Uncle stood next to it to listen to a proclamation by Günter who was dressed up as Santa Claus had made a deep impression on her. The recollection that cigars were passed out was also accurate. Latency time: 5½ months.

The remaining cases all involved Günter.

**3;10** The stay in Swinemünde was 7½ months in the past. Günter was looking in a picture book and saw a landscape with a lake and mountains. He pointed to the lake and asked if it was deep. When mother answered in the affirmative, he pointed more precisely to the edge of the lake and said, "*But it's not deep here.*" Mother: "How do you know that?" Günter (not word for word): "*Well at the beach, it wasn't deep there, either; I went into the water there and there was sand.*"

**4;1** Three months later, he again recalled Swinemünde, prompted this time by an auditory rather than visual stimulus. Specifically, the sound of the trees (blowing in the wind) brought the fall at the Baltic Sea to his mind. Perhaps he was reminded of the sound of the waves, which he expressed in his typically awkward way: "*It feels like we're in . . . Swinemünde.*" The same recollection was repeated several times later in the month, the last occasion was noted at age 4;11½, when the stay in Swinemünde was already 1¾ years in the past.

**4;4** His gaze fell onto a lamp in our bedroom. It reminded him that this lamp had been hung in the children's room in our previous apartment. By this time, we had been living in our new apartment for $1\frac{1}{2}$ years.

We come now to the recollections of colors mentioned at the beginning, both of which relate to the clothing of the same person—namely the nanny Marie, who had left when Günter was 2;3 years old.

**4;6** Mother writes, "This morning the children's current nanny put on a new blue- and white-striped blouse. Hardly had Günter seen her in the elevator when he cried out: *'You look like Marie; she had a blouse just like that.'*"

**4;11½** "For the first time, I dressed Günter's little sister Eva today in black-and-white checked frock. To that Günter said: *'Eva, you are Marie.'* Mother: 'Why do you say that?' Günter: *'Well, Marie had a frock just like that, only* (pointing to the trimming) *not that blue and that black.'* Previously, I had never been able to fully determine whether his recollections were based on the content of our discussions about Marie or if his recollections were based on his own direct experiences with her. I now obtained firm proof of the latter. In fact, during the summer in which she left us, Marie had worn a blouse that in style and color was almost identical to that being worn by the new nanny. Besides, Marie had also worn a black-and-white checked garment at that time."

Neither of these events was mentioned during the intervening periods, which were $2\frac{1}{2}$ and $2\frac{3}{4}$ years, respectively. "At the time that the nanny Marie left us, Günter could scarcely speak. He named very few things, and could not name the colors at all. None of the words that he now uses to convey his recollections was at that time in his vocabulary, and yet it was possible for everything to be implanted in his mind in a form lacking words in symbols, and reappear again later after a long time period."

Without this serendipitously observed achievement of memory we would never have thought possible this years-long retention of colors independent of language. It is possible that we are witness to an individual phenomenon. From the time that Günter was able to speak and name the colors, it became clear to us that his interest in colors was above average. When he was still younger than 3 years old he looked at landscapes and individual objects in a way that showed greater interest in their colors. The findings mentioned previously show us subsequently that, in his case, the apperception of colors began still earlier than that.

Neither in the literature nor with our other children have we encountered or made observations similar to these.[15]

**4;11½** An unexpected counter to the previously mentioned recollective achievements was provided by a gap in recollection that we likewise observed at the age of 4;11½. It had to do with an impression made not fully 2 years previously and having strong and many-faceted affective undertones but that nevertheless could not be elicited either through questioning or by mentioning things relevant to the beginning of the series of events in question. The boy, age 3;0¾, had gone with us to attend the morning rehearsal of a traveling circus. During this rehearsal, horses were being broken in. As he entered the arena, Günter became very frightened when he saw a horse running around loose. He feared that Hilde and he would be bitten. We had to take him outside to be calmed down, and then he wanted to go back inside. But then he became afraid again, and we had to go back out, and in this fashion we went back and forth, in and out, several times, until his fear slowly gave way to interest and pleasant excitement. Eventually, he even requested a live horse as a gift, and during the next days preferred to play circus. Now one would think that affective experiences on such a scale as this would not fail to make a lasting impression on the child's mind, especially a child whose strong and enduring ability to form impressions is apparent from the findings reported previously—we were all the more surprised when 23 months later he seemed to have retained nothing at all of these experiences. The entire event seems to have been erased. How limited is the ability of adults to judge which impressions have the special qualities necessary for them to become a lasting part of the child's memory!

It is apparent from what was said previously that Günter's recollections are primarily of a visual nature. Usually, it is not possible to determine how vivid and how precise a child's visual image might be. Yet with Günter, insight into this matter is facilitated by the fact that he draws a great deal, and indeed does so from memory. At the age of 5½, he could draw many kinds of animals, from the elephant to the June bug. Most of the drawings are quite accurate images based on recollections of the outlines of pictures he has often seen.[16]

5;4½   Through his drawings, we are sometimes led to other recollections of his, too. Thus he once sketched the Schneegruben Inn, in which the shape of the tower was quite accurate, a not-very-pointed pyramid.

"When the topic of the tower came up at mealtime, Hilde described it incorrectly as "four-sided"—in other words, having a flat roof, and Günter outdid her. He said that the tower has a point, but one not as pointed as that of another church in the area. From his drawing and description one can infer how clear his visual recollection was. At the time of this incident, our stay in Schreiberhau (where the Schneegruben Inn is always in view) had ended 16 months previously.

At about 5;6 Günter showed a great interest in numbers. He would read aloud those he saw on houses, electric-powered trains, and license plates. Even though he did not necessarily mean to memorize the numbers, those that he read were impressed into his memory.

**5;6**   For example, mother asked him once if he still knew the number that his sister had on her train ticket yesterday. He promptly said it correctly: 22-9-66, just as he had recited it the previous day while looking at the number. In the meantime, he had read many numbers on other houses and trains (most of them having two or three digits) without any resulting confusion. Presumably, we are seeing the joint effects of auditory–motor and visual components, but—as is characteristic of the boy more in general—the latter are playing the larger role.[17]

**5;6½**   Another recollection involving color—even though only a short interval of time was involved—happened on the occasion of the Kaiser's birthday. The electric cars traveled around during the day decorated with little flags of many different kinds. In the evening, when he began telling us about this, we asked him about the colors and he answered immediately: "*white and black, white and yellow, white and red.*" He was correct: Those are the colors of Prussia, Silesia, and Breslau.

**5;5**   One morning in bed, Günter produced an entire set of recollections stemming from different times but having the same central theme. He had spent the night with his parents after a tonsillectomy. When he awakened fully rested and found himself in a good mood because of the unusual extent to which he was being pampered, he began to rattle off recollections that related to mother's previous three birthdays. Among other things, he said, "*On your birthday I was in my wagon and had a garland on, and Hilde and Eva were going around with garlands and, I think, bouquets in their hands, and daddy rode me into the birthday room and Hilde and Eva went into the dining room.*" This birthday event took place about 2¾ years ago. At that time Günter was 2;8—in the meantime nothing more about this event had been said. By our recollections, Günter was correct on those matters concerning himself, but he was mistaken about little sister Eva. At that time, she was only a few weeks old and so would not have been able to participate actively. Günter is just in the habit of naming his little sister as a participant in all common undertakings, and he did so this time, too, in an instance in which he was not correct.

There followed another reminiscence: "*Once on your birthday, I went around holding the moon and the sun.*" Mother: "Who had the moon?" "*Hilde had the sun and I had the moon.*" Mother: "What were they fastened to?"

"*To the hobby horses.*" "What were they made of?" "*Cardboard.*" "What did they look like?" "*Silver.*" "Both of them?" "*Yes.*"

This account, too, which related to the birthday that had occurred 1¾ years previously, was correct in all details save the last: the moon was covered with silver paper, but the sun was covered with gold paper. But it is noteworthy that the error in this instance was elicited by our own questions.

Similarly, he also brought to mind his last birthday, which had occurred 9 months previously. The children wore animal masks.

We noted additional recollections with latency times from 1 to 2 years during the boy's sixth year, but they do not reveal anything essentially new.

# 6

## PURPOSIVE RECALL

In most of the small child's recollections, the will plays no role, either because the recollections surface freely or because they are reactions to external promptings. The will, which in the child is otherwise so prominent, develops in this area relatively late. The reason for this is that when it comes to recollection, the will must be oriented not toward outer activities, as is true in other domains, but instead toward internal psychological processes, and for the child to do this his or her preoccupation with outer-directed activities must be curtailed.[18]

Purposive recall involves, first, the noticing of a gap; second, the belief that one will be able to fill that gap; and third, the effort to achieve that end. To willfully recall something, one must concentrate, isolate one's self from distractions, and be able to fix one's self inwardly on the ideational complex in question. That alone is a formidable task for the child, one that she or he is able to cope with completely only from about the fourth year on. But this concentration is only a part of the completely developed will to recall. In many cases, the adult does not limit him- or herself to this, but instead positively strives, with all available means, to retrieve the sought-after ideational contents from the deep. The adult actively seeks, and the small child only waits. The child still does not have the wherewithal to gradually approximate the sought-after material through combinations and reconstructions of relevant circumstances. The child is not able to retrieve a forgotten name by proceeding, as the adult does, from

65

the still-known first syllable or from an approximate sound or from the similarity to another name. We do not yet know the precise point in development at which the child begins to make systematic use of these aids to purposive recall. This probably does not happen until the later grades of elementary school. (It is, by the way, really not so much a matter of will as of intellect.) In any case, during the period of childhood with which we are concerned, purposive recall is only present in the more passive form mentioned earlier.

The literature offers virtually nothing on the topic of purposive recall. An exception to this is the work of Major [1906, pp. 223–224], who treated the problem rather thoroughly. According to him, the first achievements in the area of purposive recall appear in the third year of life.

**2;3** With his son, Major did experiments on his recollection of shapes by presenting to the child various geometric shapes along with their names and in subsequent days testing to see if the names of the shapes could be recalled when he pointed to them. In these cases, he undoubtedly observed purposive recollection. He depicted in some detail the facial expressions involved. Early on, the boy's facial expressions were similar to those of an adult who is trying to find a name. At first, the child grimaced. He showed his teeth, closed his eyes, and so forth. Major determined that it was not this grimacing but rather a relaxed posture with held breath and a slightly opened mouth that proved most favorable to purposive recall. "In the latter case it seemed as if the child was waiting for the coming name, as if he knew that he knew it and was trying to call it up." Major conveyed further how his question about the name of a shape made the gap in the ideational sequence feel pleasantly palpable to the boy. "When the gap was filled, and the missing element of the sequence was found, a great pleasure came over him, which expressed itself in the joyful way in which the sought-after name was spoken. Often he would dance with pleasure and repeat the word over and over again."

We did not observe purposive recall at such an early age as this, possibly because at the time our observations were not directed toward this particular aspect of the problem. Nevertheless, we once explicitly mentioned such an achievement in Hilde's case around the end of the third year. She recognized her grandmother and, after pausing a moment to think, named her "*gramma*" (cf. p. 8).

**2;8** The Scupins [1907] report the following of their son at about this same age: "When he was asked about a missing key, he at first thought hard about it, then said, '*Ask Sohni.*' But Sohni also knew nothing about the key, and when we turned once again to the boy, he thought about it again and then said with conviction: '*The spider ate the key all up.*'" Here the question was not really one of purposive recall, because we found out later that the boy had had nothing to do with the missing key and therefore had no material to recall. The "concentration" was in this instance simply an effect of the suggestive question.

Prior to the conclusion of the third year, events of this sort are surely rare. In the fourth year they occur somewhat more often. From this age, we have a diary entry concerning Eva.

3;5 "The children were talking about the various doctors who often come to us, and many names were mentioned. I asked Eva: 'What is the name of the 'uncle' doctor who always makes you well?' She thought about this intently. One could see how she was searching for the name. Desperately she gave the name of another doctor, and she was visibly relieved when I told her the correct name." We did the same test at age 3;7 and had the opportunity to observe her expressive movement. She raised her head, looked at the ceiling with wide-open eyes, and stayed immobile in this position for a long time. But this time, too, she failed to find the name, even though it was a name that she had known a long time and had often heard said.

3;6 Here is another example. One day when we were departing on a trip, Eva had been playing in the room where an open, small suitcase stood. Later, when the suitcase had been snapped shut, we found ourselves missing the key and asked the child: "Did you have the key?" Eva immediately and very confidently answered in the affirmative, and went looking for it. She ran into the next room, but quickly returned, because she had apparently thought about the matter: "*Maybe I didn't have it.*" Suddenly, while she was still walking around looking, she called, "*I put it into the white suitcase.*" We asked, pointing to the smaller suitcase, which is brown on the outside, "In this one?" Eva: "*No.*" In spite of this, we suspected that she did mean that bag, which is light-colored on the inside, opened it, and discovered we were correct. At this point she recognized the bag, and pointed to a lining pocket. Inside was the key.

We have on hand two additional cases from Hilde's fourth year. At the age of 3;10 she corrected a mistake after further thought (see p. 29). A later diary entry ran as follows:

3;11 We were speaking of travels, and it occurred to Hilde that we had eaten something in the train. "*We ate in the train, didn't we?*" Mother: "What kind of meat?" Hilde: "*I don't know.*" Mother: "Think about it, perhaps it will come to you." Hilde (after a brief period of thought): "*Cutlets?*" She was correct. Moreover, the pleasure that she took in being able to remember so excited her that she began to relate all manner of recollections. The latency time in this instance was 7 months. To be sure, we had on occasion spoken of this trip in the meantime, but there had been no discussion about the food."

In subsequent years the child became increasingly able to remember things at will. Unfortunately, we do not have any notes from the 5th and 6th years concerning this ability, which we ourselves observed. Friedrich [1906, p. 33] cites a negative case: A boy is asked, "Do you know any other boys?" Answer: "*I don't know anyone: I only know my brothers and sisters.*" Elaborating, Friedrich said, "When the boy is trying to call something to mind, the pressure to answer narrows his field of vision to such an extent that he cannot think of one other boy whom he knows. The larger the role memory plays in psychological development in early childhood, the greater must be the limitations of purposive recall in the moment that the available contents of memory are to be used."

Without doubt, it can happen in isolated cases that a question that surprises a child can result in a kind of constraint and in this way hinder the child's ability to bring certain material to mind. However, it would be completely false to suggest that this is what generally happens at this age. The very fact that at 6 years old the child is considered ready for school contraindicates this view, because one of the very first psychological activities that the school must require and presume to be present is the child's ability to willfully recall the material that is being taught.

**6;1**  Just after Günter had completed his sixth year he gave us an opportunity to record an instance of willful recall. Mother had said to the children: "Remind me tomorrow to send out the hammock for mending." On the next day, mother remembered that she had asked the children to remind her of something, but could not remember what it was. So she asked the children: "What were you supposed to remind me about?" Hilde tried without success to remember, but Günter's effort to remember was successful.

# 7

## MISTAKEN RECOLLECTIONS

As we showed in chapter 3, false testimonies by young children can range from the completely unconscious mistaken recollection, to fantastic accounts that are illusory, to various forms of pseudo-lies, all the way to genuine, deliberate lies. To the degree that the literature contains any material at all concerning the appearance of these phenomena in early childhood[19] it is limited almost exclusively to the latter endpoint of this spectrum—in other words, to the lie—and to that which is understood as lying. For this reason, we must once again rely primarily on our own material in discussing the other phenomena.

The first genuinely false testimonies (compare the report on Hilde, p. 10) emerge when a child is unable to locate an actual experience at the correct point of time in the past. With our other (two) children, we were able to register incidents fully parallel to those we mentioned previously.

**2;4** "Today, and also in recent days, Günter returned from his daily walk claiming incorrectly: 'Met Annie 'n Mary.' These are two children with whom Günter has made friends, and whom he previously saw often, but not in the past 2 weeks. Actually, I regard the apparent spontaneity of this testimony as a consequence of my customary question to the little caravan on its return home: 'Did you all meet anyone?' Günter has already given a false answer (several times) under the suggestive influence of this question, and now he gives his report before I ask the question."

That apparent spontaneity can occur deserves attention in other cases, too, because even among older children and adults something that is at first elicited only by suggestion can gradually take on a spontaneous form and as such be evaluated psychologically as something other than what it is.

**3;5**   We have made another observation of Eva's temporal confusion. In the morning, the children had taken a walk with their mother to the mountain called *Kinderzobten* and finally ended up at the home of a family we know. (Ten days earlier, both parents had accompanied the children on a similar walk, on which occasion we did not go to the *Kinderzobten* but did again end up at the home of the same family.) Later at dinner, when the discussion turned to the walk that had taken place that day, father said jokingly to the children: "You children have it good. You can go on walks and pick flowers and I have to work." At that, Eva said, "*But you were with us, too.*" In the face of further questioning, she stubbornly insisted on this claim. Not until we had discussed the matter a long time did she surrender halfway: "*You weren't at the Kinderzobten, but only with the St's.*" But gradually it seemed to dawn on her that not even the second part of her claim was true in this instance, and she declared that she had only been joking in what she said.

**4;6**   A false testimony that we observed on the part of Günter had an entirely different basis. At midday, the following exchange took place. Mother: "Where is Eva's mush spoon? Did she throw it away again?" Günter: "*Yes, she threw it away.*" Mother (forcefully): "Did you see it happen?" Günter: "*I didn't see it, but I see that it's not here, and so I know it.*" So in this case, something that the boy suspects is expressed as a certainty. Had we not asked him pointedly about this, then it would have remained a certainty for him. So at $4\frac{1}{2}$ years, the boy was self-critical enough to admit that he had not actually perceived something, and sufficiently logical to deduce the consequences of that. Nevertheless, the expression "*therefore I know it*" shows how, to the naive child, "having an opinion" and "knowing" are the same.

**5;6½**   With no external prompting at all, and so from the perspective of an observer what seems to be a "freely occurring" way, Günter had a recollection of a picture that up until 9 months previously had been hanging continuously in the children's bedroom, but then had been removed and not mentioned again. From the start, his first question about the picture contained gross errors, and when we tried to study his recollection more closely, we found a mixture of correct and incorrect statements. Because we were able to record part of the exchange stenographically, we relate it in detail.

The event has to do with a large charcoal sketch of a "Grandfather picture"[20]; the mistakes are indicated by wide-spaced type (see Table 4). At first Günter asked quite spontaneously where the picture was in which the grandmother was feeding the boy and in which there was a dog. Un-

### TABLE 4
#### Günter's Recollections of "Picture of Grandfather"

| Mother | Günter | Observations |
|---|---|---|
| | Grandfather was there and a cat and a boy, and the grandfather was on a stool and the boy was standing up. | |
| Anything else? | A pussycat | |
| Where? | Next to the t a b l e --- Next to the stool, where the boy s a t | Corrects himself immediately |
| Wasn't he standing? | Yes, where the boy stood. | |
| What did grandfather have on his head? | Grandfather had a bonnet on. | (He means cap) |
| What did it look like? | R e d . | |
| Was it a colorful picture? | Yes, I think so. | (In an uncertain tone) |
| What color was the bonnet? | Don't know. | |
| What was the grandfather doing? | Gave the boy soup. | |
| From what? | From a plate. | |
| Where was the plate? | The grandfather was holding it in his hand. | |
| With what was he feeding the boy? | A wooden spoon. | |
| Were there other colors in the picture? | All of it was colorful. Y e l l o w  s p o o n, a l i t t l e b i t  b r o w n i s h, pussycat was black and white. | |
| How was the boy dressed? | B l u e shirt and black pants and b l o n d hair. | (Here he laughed, embarrassed, because hair is not part of clothing.) |
| Did he have something on his head? | N o . | |
| How was grandfather dressed? | I think he had on only black— I'm sure. | |

fortunately, his older sister chimed in immediately to correct him, saying that the grandmother was actually a grandfather and the dog was actually a cat. With this help, he proceeded as [shown in Table 4] (errors are space-typed):

We then showed him a smaller version of the same picture, but he demanded to see the original, saying, "*But the big picture was colored, I think.*" When it was placed before him, he was especially surprised that the cap was not red.

The errors that occurred are of a dual nature. On the one hand they are related to the colors. Apparently, his recollections were contaminated by farm house pictures very familiar to him from picture books. For example, one of these pictures that has very vivid colors shows a farm boy sitting at the table and eating, with a dog next to him. The color of the wooden spoon is indeed that of the kitchen spoon he has in fact often seen. The boy's clothing could be a mixture of reminiscences from many colorfully portrayed farm boys. The colorfulness extends also to the red cap and becomes increasingly plausible to him, though the added "*I think*" proves that a shred of doubt remains.

This case of ours is different from the experimental studies with pictures that have been conducted thus far in that the recollection was related not to a one-time presentation but instead to something present to the boy on a continuous basis. From his 2nd until nearly the end of his 5th year of life, Günter had seen the picture almost daily. The strong impression that must have been made by this was nonetheless blurred by the 9-month absence of the picture, and errors were able to creep into his account.[21]

**5;7½**  At the age of 5;7½, Günter provided a truly paradigmatic example of a testimony given in good faith, yet grossly false, regarding something that had just happened. "At the table, he had been playing with a wallet that he had just been given as a gift, along with some play money. After the meal, he ran into the adjoining children's room and returned glumly a few minutes later: his play money had disappeared, and he just could not find it. Mother: 'Where did you put it down?' He answered promptly: '*On the children's table*' (in the children's room). Because I (mother) assumed that he had taken the play money with him out of the room, I said, 'Well, go sit at the children's table and try to remember where you went from there.' But he knew this without going to sit at the table: '*To the window.*' To the next question, whether he had taken the play money with him to the window, he answered yes, but he was not so sure. I had him go over to the window sill and look. No luck. While he looked in the vicinity of the window, I discovered the play money, all laid out neatly in order, at the place at the table where he had been sitting for lunch. He had left the play money lying there when he ran off. At first I said nothing to him, but called him to me and suggested, 'Now think hard, did you take the play money with you into the children's room after eating.' A certain, '*Yes, I* *know just where*' was his answer. 'Where did you set the play money down?' '*On the table.*' 'And then?' '*On the window sill.*' 'Are you absolutely sure?' '*I can't say absolutely sure, but I think so.*' This 'I think so' related only to the window sill; regarding the table he was firmly convinced. Now I led him to his place at the table, and his expression mirrored great amazement. I used this occasion to incorporate a kind of age-appropriate "testimony pedagogy" (see chapter 11).

The origin of this mistake is not entirely clear. Perhaps he had played with the money at the table before eating and then mistakenly thought that he had left it there rather than taken it somewhere else before mealtime. But perhaps affect played a role, too: He might have assumed from the beginning that he could not have permitted himself to be separated from his much-loved money, and now looked for it where he would have put it had he kept it with him continuously.

The next instance is instructive because it shows that a clear discrepancy can occasionally exist between recollection and memory. As already mentioned on p. 62, Günter's drawings are based for the most part on memories in the form of vivid visual images from pictures he has seen. However:

**5;8** Once he drew a picture of two elephants on the easel, a large one with the trunk pointed down and a small one with the trunk raised high. Behind them were two rather large palm trees. When we asked him if he had ever seen anything similar to this, he recalled a picture postcard in his collection, but added immediately: "*But there were no palm trees in the postcard.*" We then compared his drawing with the postcard. The latter showed elephants with their trunks positioned as in Günter's sketch, and also in the background, two tiny palm trees. Günter was amazed when we pointed these out to him.

So while he was making his drawing, the picture he had seen previously was exerting an effect without his being conscious of it. In this instance we have memory without recollection. His subsequent recollection included only the elephants and negated the palm trees. Again, we have a valid memory coincident with a false recollection. Some additional mistakes of recollection that occasionally crept into our son's reminiscences about birthdays have already been mentioned (pp. 63–64). Others will be discussed in the next chapter.

# 8

# EXPERIMENTAL STUDIES OF TESTIMONY IN EARLY CHILDHOOD

Many studies of testimony have been done with schoolchildren using pictures. These studies have typically entailed presenting a child with an unfamiliar picture to investigate the effect of a one-time, temporally circumscribed exposure. Even the first experiments of this kind carried out with children younger than 6 years of age (by Lipmann and Wendriner [1906][22] followed this approach.

The few studies of testimony that we carried out with our children were designed to compare performance at three different ages. For this reason, the sequence of investigations was kept as similar as possible for all three children.

Like the experiments carried out with schoolchildren, one group of our experiments involved single exposures. A second group of experiments was concerned with capabilities for recalling material that had been exposed repeatedly or more or less continuously. So far as we know, such studies have not previously been carried out experimentally.

## STUDIES INVOLVING MATERIAL PRESENTED ONCE

In the first group of experiments, we could not use the pictures that have been used in previous experiments of this sort because our children were already familiar with those pictures from the books of illustrations by Walters. For this reason, we chose instead the "Breakfast picture" (Figure 1) used by Marie Dürr-Borst [1906] for testimony experiments with children. Even so, this picture bears a certain similarity, in terms of mood and situation portrayed, to some in the aforementioned book of illustrations, a fact that had some influence in the case of our youngest child.

In the cases of Hilde and Günter, we presented the picture on in-

Figure 1.

dependent occasions but in the same way. In Eva's case, we had to modify the procedure somewhat because of her younger age.

Each of the two older children silently inspected the picture for 1 minute. Then, each child had to report on the contents of the picture. Questioning according to a predesigned list followed. Seven days later, each child was asked to give a secondary report on the contents of the picture without the picture being presented again. Finally, there was a session of self-correction, carried out with the help of the picture, which was once again presented. In the meantime, the children had not spoken about the picture, and indeed had scarcely thought any more about it.

We present the sequence of questioning for each child separately. Primary and secondary testimonies are given alongside one another. The questioning session included only questions about those aspects of the picture that had not been spontaneously mentioned in the child's report. As can be seen, the questions listed under "Questioning" in the first set of findings relate sometimes to the primary testimony, sometimes to the secondary, and most often to both.

The frequencies obtained for correct, false, and indeterminate statements in the report and during questioning are summarized in an overview table (see Table 5). To facilitate replications of the respective experiments, we have provided appendixes [A and B] of results at the end of the book. These contain the analysis of each separate statement.

In discussing the individual statements we present only noteworthy results.

For Hilde's primary testimony there is comparable material from children of approximately the same age [U. Stein, 1904, pp. 125 & 140]. In comparison with these children, Hilde appears advanced. In their respective reports, the comparable 7-year-old school girls were all in the "substantive stage": They report only the seen objects, and say nothing of activities, relationships, or attributes. In contrast, Hilde's report contains all categories, even some exact portrayals of attributes and statements about colors, and this is true to an extent that to date has been reported in testimony experiments only among older children. By way of explanation it is relevant to point out that from an early age the child was accustomed to looking at pictures attentively and to discussing their contents with her mother.

The two errors in the report consist of a confusion (between the colors of the dress and the apron) and an exaggeration (chairs instead of a single chair).

During questioning Hilde made 42 statements, of which 33 were correct and 9 were incorrect (accuracy = 78½%). Her suggestibility was slight. In response to the various leading questions (about butter, lace, hem of the apron, knife in the woman's hand, barefootedness of the boy, window) she always answered in the negative. On the other hand, questions about

## TABLE 5
## Breakfast Picture: Hilde (7;8)

| Report | |
|---|---|
| Primary report | Secondary report (7 days later) |
| The woman has brown hair. And the boy is eating bread and sits at the table. The woman is standing. Lying next to the stool is a red bookbag. The stools are made almost entirely of straw, except for wooden holes. And a big case stands against the wall, also made of wood. And the woman had a blue apron on and a red dress. Right? | The woman had a blue dress and a red apron. On the wash basin there was a flower pot. And the boy is eating bread. The woman is about to cut. Both have brown hair. I can no longer remember what kind of pants the boy had on. I know: blue jacket and red pants, right? The woman is standing. And next to the boy is a bookbag, but one cannot see the straps at the back. The bag has red cover flap. One cannot see the wash basin entirely. I don't remember anything else. |

| Questioning | | |
|---|---|---|
| Questions | Primary | Secondary |
| On what side was the woman? | (Points to the right) | (Points to the right) |
| What is the woman doing? | *She is cutting bread.* | |
| Does the apron have lace around the edges? | *No.* | *No.* |
| What form does the apron have? | *Almost has shoulders, but doesn't.* | *Pinned on here, nearly with shoulders.* |
| Does one see the woman from the front or from the side? | *From the side.* | *From the side.* |
| What is in her hand? | *Nothing—bread.* | *Bread, it is on the table and she is grasping it.* |
| Does she have a knife in her hand? | *No, it is lying on the table.* | *No, it is lying on the table.* |
| How does the bread look? | *Brown, as usual.* | *Brown, as usual.* |
| Is it whole or sliced? | *Sliced.* | *Sliced.* |
| Is there a table? | *Yes.* | |
| Color? | *Brown.* | *Brown.* |
| Form? | *Square.* | *Square.* |

TABLE 5   (*Continued*)

| | Questioning | |
|---|---|---|
| Questions | Primary | Secondary |
| What is lying or standing on top? | *Bread and knife.* (M.: I thought that the woman had the bread in her hand.) *A little bit is still on the table.* | *Knife and bread.* |
| Isn't there butter too? | *No.* | *No, I think not.* |
| How is the boy dressed? | *Brown jacket and brown pants, I think, or blue; no, I think brown.* | |
| Isn't he barefoot? | *No.* | *He only has socks on.* |
| Color of his socks? | *Red.* | *Red.* |
| Is he wearing shoes? | | *No.* |
| What kind of shoes? | *Small shoes, brown.* | |
| What is he sitting on? | *On a stool.* | *On a stool.* |
| How are his feet placed? | *Hanging down.* | *Crossed over one another.* |
| Hair color? | *Brown.* | |
| How do the slices of bread look? | *Half off of the plate.* | |
| How is he holding them? | (She spreads thumb and index finger.) | (She spreads thumb and index finger.) |
| Can we see the boy from the front or from the side? | *From the side.* | *From the side.* |
| What can we see of the room? | *Door and trunk.* | *On the trunk is a flowerpot with red flowers, green leaves. No window. The door is open. Nothing else.* (M.: You just said trunk; before you said chest.) *Chest is wrong.* |
| Is the door open or shut? | *Shut.* | |
| Has it 1 or 2 panels? | *One.* | *One.* |

*Table continues*

TABLE 5   (*Continued*)

| | Questioning | |
|---|---|---|
| Questions | Primary | Secondary |
| Is there no window to be seen? | *Yes—no, no.* | *No.* |
| On which side is the trunk? | (Points right.) | (Points right.) |
| Is it entirely visible? | *No, the woman is standing in front.* | (M.: Why can't one see the trunk entirely?)<br>*One can see it entirely.* |
| Is anything on top? | *No.* (M.: Isn't there a flowerpot on top?) *No.* | |
| What kind of flowers? | | *Tulips or something like that.* |
| Are the straps on the bookbag visible? | *No, they are in back.* | |
| Is there anything else on the floor? | *No.* | *Yes.* |
| Is there a mug to be seen? | *No.* | *Under the table.* |
| Where? | | |
| How many handles does it have? | | *One.* |
| Color of the mug? | | *Blue and white, I think.* |
| Isn't there a cover on top? | (Self-correction after looking at the picture again:) *I was correct that there was no top, but the mug is green. And the straps are visible. The woman is standing in front of the trunk. I said that the boy had a blue jacket and it is green.* (M.: Look at the feet.) *He has shoes.* (M.: What kind of socks?) *Blue.* | *No.* |

two objects that were actually present, the jug and the flowerpot, were also answered in the negative. Among the answers to questions about color, more than half were false. She guessed at about half of the colors, which she had not observed with conscious attentiveness. With regard to the bookbag, Hilde's testimony was an amalgamation of correct perception and false interpretation: She knew correctly that the straps hung to the back, but concluded falsely that for this reason they would not be visible. Apparently, she imagined that the front of the bag rather than its side was turned toward the onlooker.

From a psychological standpoint, the secondary account given by Hilde is noteworthy for the fact that it is better than the first account. It was surely a coincidence that the misspecification of the colors of the woman's clothing was subsequently corrected. Moreover, the flowerpot, which had been firmly denied in the first report, was spontaneously mentioned 8 days later, and during questioning after the second report, the flowers in the pot were identified correctly. Similarly, the mug whose existence had been denied in the first report surfaced during questioning after the second report. It thus seems as if memoric images can undergo a period up and down, so one might not be conscious of them even immediately after perception but then conscious of them again during some later reproduction of the memories.

So for the two named objects we find a contradiction between the primary and secondary reports. A further contradiction occurs within the second account, between the report itself and what is said during questioning. Spontaneously, H. said, "*The chest* (= case) *cannot be seen entirely*," and in response to the question: "Why can't we see all of it?" she answered surprisingly, "*We can see all of it*." It is possible that in this instance she thought she had been asked a leading question and opposed the intended suggestion. In general, Hilde's resistance to suggestion was effective later as well as earlier. She resisted all four leading questions. The only evidence that her recollections were somewhat less clear lies in the fact that in the secondary report she was less certain than she had previously been in her denial of the existence of the butter ("*No, I don't think so*").

After the conclusion of the second report we showed her the picture so that she could correct herself. Four errors (not quite half of all of them) were spontaneously corrected.

**5;5** Günter, who is 2½ years younger than Hilde, delivered an account that, all things considered, is about equal to that of his older sister. (See Table 6.) His report is just as comprehensive, in terms of content almost as detailed, and does not contain more errors. During questioning, his report is about equal to hers in terms of correct statements, though his report does contain more mistakes. Still, this greater inaccuracy is limited to the

## TABLE 6
### Breakfast Picture: Günter (5;5)

| Report | |
|---|---|
| **Primary report** | **Secondary report (7 days later)** |
| I could see a boy. He was sitting at the table and was eating bread. And there was also a knife on the table where the woman had cut off a piece of bread. And next to the woman there was what you find in a kitchen, a kind of bench. And there was a flowerpot on top with flowers. And the door in the room was open. (M.: Anything else?) Oh, yes: And the woman was standing and the boy was sitting on the chair. | Door was open and window. (M.: Could you see a window?) Yes, and stuff you see in a kitchen—like a crate with a flowerpot with palagonias on it. And there was a table in the room. And next to it a chair and a boy sitting on it eating bread. And the boy's mother is cutting the bread. (M.: Is she really cutting the bread?) Yes. On the floor under the stool is a broken pot. (M.: What else?) There is a bookbag lying on the floor. |

| Questioning | | |
|---|---|---|
| **Questions** | **Primary** | **Secondary** |
| On which side was the woman and on which the boy? | | *On the right side.* |
| Is the woman standing or sitting? | | *Standing.* |
| What is she doing? | *She's looking at the bread.* | *Cutting bread.* |
| Color of her clothing? | *Skirt red.* | *Red skirt, blue apron with white stripes.* |
| Does she have an apron? | *Yes.* | |
| Does it have a lace hem? | *I don't know.* | *No.* |
| Color of the apron? | *Blue.* | |
| Kind of apron? | *Shoulder straps.* | *Square.* |
| Color of the woman's hair? | *Blonde.* | *Blonde.* |
| Do we see her from the front or the side? | *From the side.* | *From the side.* |
| What does she have in her hand? | *Nothing—the bread.* | *Well, a knife—no, nothing.* (M.: I think she is cutting the bread. With what?) *I'm sure she's just resting.* (M.: So, she doesn't have a knife?) *No.* |
| Does she have a knife in her hand? | *No, it is on the table.* | |
| How does the bread look? | *Brown, long.* | |

TABLE 6 (*Continued*)

| Questions | Primary | Secondary |
|---|---|---|
| Is it whole or sliced? | *Sliced.* | *Sliced.* |
| Is a table visible? | *Yes.* | |
| Color? | *A little bit yellow.* | *Yellow.* |
| Shape? | *Square.* | *Square.* |
| What is on the table? | *A knife—just a knife.* | *Knife and bread.* |
| Isn't there butter there, too? | *No.* | *No.* |
| Is the boy standing or sitting? | | *He is sitting.* |
| What is he wearing? | *I don't know.* | *Blue and white striped shirt and red pants. Black shoes.* |
| Color of the jacket? | *Blue.* | |
| Color of the pants? | *Black, I think.* | |
| Isn't he barefoot? | *No, black shoes and brown socks, I think.* | |
| Color of the socks? | | *Brown, I think.* |
| Boots or shoes? | *Boots.* | |
| On what is he sitting? | *A stool.* | *A stool.* |
| How is he holding his feet? | *I don't know.* | *There's one of these, and he's resting his feet there.* |
| What is he doing? | *He is eating.* | *He is eating bread.* |
| His hair color? | *Black, I think, or blonde.* | *Blonde.* |
| What do the slices of bread look like? | *White and brown.* | |
| How is he holding the bread? | *(Holds thumb and index finger together.)* | *So. (Holds thumb and index finger together.)* |
| Do we see him from the front or the side? | *From the side.* | *From the side.* |
| Does the door have one or two panels? | *One.* | *One.* |
| Can one see out? | *Nothing.* | *No.* |
| Isn't there a window? | *Yes.* | |
| What side is it on? | *Here (he points to the left)—or no. Yes, here, I think.* | *(He points to the left.)* |

*Table continues*

TABLE 6 (*Continued*)

| Questions | Primary | Secondary |
|---|---|---|
| Can one see through? | *A flowerpot, I think.* | *Trees or flowers.* |
| Is the window open or closed? | | *Open.* |
| Are there gardenias on it? | | *Yes, I think so—or no.* |
| Is that a real bench that is next to the woman? | *Like in the kitchen.* | |
| Which side is it on? | (He points to the right.) | |
| Does it have feet? | *Yes, four.* | |
| Can we see it entirely? | *A little bit hidden; there is no more paper.* | *No.* (M.: Why not?) *It should be wider.* |
| What kind of flowers are in the pot? | *I don't know any-more.* | |
| Have you seen them before? | *Yes, at the Kaiser-Wilhelm Place.* | |
| Don't you know their name? | *Geraniums.* | |
| Color of the flowers? | *Red.* | |
| Color of the pot? | *Little bits of pink.* | *Dark red. Some of it bright red.* |
| Is there a saucer underneath it? | *No, I don't think so.* | *No.* |
| What is on the floor? | *Under the stool, a broken coffee pot.* | |
| How many handles does the mug have? | *One.* | *Two.* |
| Color of the mug? | *White and blue.* | *White with blue.* |
| Isn't there a top on it? | *Yes.* | *Yes.* |
| Its color? | *White and blue.* | *Also white and blue.* |
| Is a bookbag visible? | *Yes.* | *Yes.* |
| Where? | *Next to the stool.* | *On the floor, here.* (points to the left.) |
| What does it look like? | *Brown.* | *Brown.* |
| Does it have another color? | | *A mirror in the mid-dle.* |

TABLE 6    (*Continued*)

Self-correction on additional presentation of the picture

*The pot isn't like that; it is green. But I was right about the pants. The pot has no top.*
(M.: What else did you say about the pot?)
*It had a top.*
(G. now lists the things he had said correctly. M.: Look again; isn't there something else you said incorrectly?)
*Oh, she has the bread in her hands! Oh, the crate ends here. Even here* (pointing to the right side of the crate) *there is still some picture.*
(M.: You've said a lot that is not in the picture at all.)
*Window!*

domains of the two more difficult categories of (a) questions about color and (b) leading questions.[23]

In his report, Günter also surpasses the "substantive stage," and indeed even the "action stage." He includes various attributes (door open, pot broken) and a great many spatial relations. Spontaneous statements concerning color are lacking, which is the rule according to general observations concerning psychological development at this age, but in Günter's case this is surprising because otherwise he has shown an extraordinarily lively interest in colors. In contrast to this experiment, another one with a picture, to be discussed further later, resulted in many spontaneous statements about color. The discrepancy could perhaps be explained as follows. To cope with the elements of the previously unfamiliar picture within the short time of a minute, the boy had too much to do, and there was no time or energy left over for conscious attention to colors. He noticed and retained colors, as is shown by the results obtained during questioning, but because his attention during original observation was not concentrated on colors, they were entirely absorbed into the material content of the picture during the spontaneous account. In the case of the picture to be discussed later, which was continuously present to Günter over a period of years, he had time enough to satisfy his interest in the content and, beyond that, to attend intensively to the colors. In this respect, he is quite different from his sister, who in the case of the latter picture was rather unobservant of colors, whereas in the case of the once-presented picture, she included colors in her rapid observations concerning the contents.[24]

In his report, Günter was not satisfied merely to report the bare facts directly visible. Instead, he went beyond the facts to give an interpretation, though this interpretation was developed quite logically from the facts: "*And there was also a knife on the table,* (with) *which the woman had sliced the bread.*" The secondary report to be discussed more later shows how the recollection was subsequently falsified through this interpretation. It is apparent both from the questioning and from the (spontaneous) report that the content was observed quite closely but the colors less so. In response to questioning about color, Günter gave seven correct and five and a half incorrect answers. He was not as resistant to leading questions as was Hilde: Three times he resisted, twice he submitted (concerning the window and the lid on the mug). It is clear that with regard to the window he was not entirely sure. (In all likelihood, the origin of his claim about the window lies in the "Farmhouse picture" from Walter's illustration book.)

In Günter's case, the primary questioning twice prompted the answer "*I don't know*," which otherwise occurred neither in his secondary questioning nor in the questioning of his sister. The rarity of this answer among small children shows how readily questions put to them are understood as challenges to take a specific position on some matter.

As was true of Hilde, the secondary account given by Günter 7 days later shows no deterioration relative to the primary account. But with regard to content some noteworthy displacements have occurred. The window that was suggested during the primary questioning and at the time still weakly doubted was mentioned spontaneously in the second report as a firm fact. On the other hand, a gap left in the primary questioning was later filled in correctly. In response to the question: "How is the boy holding his feet? G. had initially answered, "*I don't know*," later he said, "*There is one of these* [a slat between the front legs of the chair] *and he is holding his feet there.*" However, it may be that the initial failure was more a matter of linguistic convenience. It is often difficult for Günter to name things he does not encounter regularly, as is apparent even from his secondary answer to the question.

The following item is more complicated: The knife, which during the primary account he correctly said was on the table (with the correct inference that the woman had used it to cut something) was in the secondary report first said to be in the woman's hand, and even when we put the question in such a manner as to raise doubts: "Is she really cutting?" his answer was affirmative. But during questioning, he corrected the recollection again. To the question: "What does the woman have in her hand?" the first answer was "*knife*," but after a short pause "*no, nothing*," and then no leading question could diminish his confidence in what he had said. In response to the question: "I believe she is cutting bread; with what?" he answered: "*I'm sure she's just resting.*" So once again we have contradictory accounts given by the same child within a few minutes.

For Günter, too, a self-correcting session was arranged at the end of the experiment. In the wink of an eye he discovered a third of his mistakes. Beyond that, a latent error was hidden in the questioning, which we would not have been able to notice at all without the self-correction session. When he looked at the picture, he said in amazement: "*Oh, she does have bread in her hands.*" Thus did it become clear that in speaking of the woman "who was just resting," he had unburdened her not only correctly of the knife but also falsely of the bread.

To date, no testimony experiments with 3-year-old children have been conducted. Yet such experiments are comparatively easy to set up, because looking at pictures is one of the great pleasures of childhood. Our picture experiments were not perceived by the children as experiments, and always gave them great pleasure.[25]

**2;11**  With Eva, it was not possible to carry out the experiment exactly as we had done with her two older siblings, because it is impossible to get a child of this age to look at a picture and say nothing. So in Eva's case, we presented the picture and asked if she would like to tell us everything she saw in the picture. The exposure time was 2 minutes rather than 1 minute, as had been the case for the other two children. We then took the picture away and proceeded to her report and then to the questioning.

Despite these favorable conditions, the gap between her achievements and those of her siblings was substantial. Compared with them, Eva commanded only about half as much of the material and a third of the spontaneity. Most of what she knew was not apparent until questioning (see Table 7).

The egocentrism reflected in Eva's perception of the picture is typical of young children. She interpreted the figures as persons familiar to her at home (brother and cook), though certainly she was being a bit playful in these instances.

In terms of the aforementioned stages (*things, activities, relationships, attributes*), the difference between the report she gave during and after looking at the picture is very apparent. While looking at the picture, connections between the things perceived were established, especially through activities (eating, moving about) and a relation (a bookbag for brother Günter). By contrast, her later recollection is entirely "substantive" in its quality, and arbitrarily puts any object next to any other. This behavior change can be well-explained as follows: In spontaneous recollection, unlike ongoing inspection of a picture or during questioning, there are no external points of reference available on which to base the course of her imagination. So she mentions only those things that have stood out for her and can thus surface again in recollection in isolated fashion. Here, then, we have new evidence for the fact that a child of a particular age can simultaneously be at two different developmental stages in relation to different domains of performance.[26]

The few (4) statements contained in the primary report are correct.

During questioning, something confusing to the child seems to have crept in quickly: A situation portrayed in the Walters' illustrations surfaced, in which a woman is standing at the stove and is stirring in a pot with a spoon. From this, Eva answered the question: "What is the woman doing?"

## TABLE 7
### Breakfast Picture: Eva (2;11)

| Primary report (while looking at the picture; 2 minutes) | Secondary report (4 days later) (without presenting the picture again) |
|---|---|
| *Günter is eating bread. And here is Toni.* <br> (M.: You should say everything.) | (M.: Do you remember how a few days ago I showed you a picture here at the desk? What was in that picture?) |
| *Flower.* | *Günter.* |
| *What is that?* (pointing to the bookbag) | *Toni.* |
| (M.: A bookbag.) | Mother. |
| *For the boys.* | Door. |
| *There is a cabinet.* | (M.: What else was there?) |
| *And that is a room* (pointing to the door). | Else. |
| *Where does one go in?* | *Toni.* |
| *And that is the kitchen.* | (M.: Was she there?) |
| *What is Günter eating?* | *Yes.* |
| *Bread.* | (M.: Toni and mother were there?) |
| B. After removing the picture. | Yes, and Elsie was there, too. |
| (M.: Tell me everything you saw.) | (M.: Do you know anything else?) |
| *Günter.* | Door. |
| *Toni.* | (M.: Do you know anything else?) |
| *Flower.* | *House.* |
| *Room.* | That's all that was there. |
| (M.: What else?) | |
| *Door.* | |
| (M.: What else?) | |
| *Toni.* | |
| *Günter.* | |

### Questioning

| Questions | Primary | Secondary |
|---|---|---|
| How is Günter dressed? | *Suit and pants.* | |
| Isn't he barefoot? | *Shoes, socks.* | |
| What is he sitting on? | *Stool.* | |
| What is he doing? | *He is eating bread.* | |
| How is he holding it? | *In his hand.* | |
| Is there a door in the room? | *Yes.* | |
| Open or closed? | *Open.* | *Open.* |

TABLE 7   (*Continued*)

| Questions | Primary | Secondary |
|---|---|---|
| Can we see out? | | *Yes, just some little pots.* |
| Is there a window? | *No.* | |
| Is there a little crate? | *No.* | *No.* |
| Is there a flowerpot? | *No—yes.* | *Yes, there is a flowerpot.* |
| Where is it standing? | *On a cabinet.* | |
| What is on the floor? | | *Bookbag.* |
| Is there a bookbag? | *Yes.* | |
| Where? | *Underneath, on the floor.* | |
| What does it look like? | *Like the table.* | |
| Is there a mug? | *No.* | *No.* |
| Is the woman standing or sitting? | *Standing. Günter is sitting.* | *Standing. Günter is sitting.* |
| What is the woman doing? | *She is cooking soup.* | *She was cooking soup —and the bookbag was there, too.* |
| Does she have an apron? | *Tied around.* | *Yes.* |
| What color is the apron? | *Green.* | *Green.* |
| What does she have in her hand. | *I don't know by myself.* | *A spoon for the soup.* |
| Does she have a knife in her hand? | *No.* | *No.* |
| Did she have bread in her hand? | | *Yes.* |
| Is there a table? | *Yes.* | *Yes.* |
| What is on the table? | *Bread.* | *The bread.* |
| What else? | *Nothing more at all.* | *Nothing more, but the bread is on the table.* (M.: But you said Toni made the soup.) *But it was bread.* (M.: So there was no soup there?) |
| Wasn't there butter there, too? | *No.* | *Just bread.* |

by saying: "*She is cooking soup.*" Two additional mistakes relate to colors, but we regard these as irrelevant because Eva's knowledge of the colors is not yet entirely correct. During the inspection of the picture, there were also some confusions of names. There remain, then, only two additional errors, involving things in the picture about which nothing was said. She did not know that, besides the bread, there was something else lying on the table. On direct questioning, the presence of the mug was denied. The most important kind of mistake, the inclusion of things that in fact were not there, was not to be found in Eva's case. Even our leading questions, which come close to adding such things (whether there was butter or a window) had no effect on her at all. We have also observed in the course of daily life that Eva is not very suggestible.

The results of the primary questioning were 26 correct answers, against which we found no false additions; 1 confusion; and 2 incorrect negations.

For the secondary questioning we also had to deviate somewhat from the procedure that had been used with the two older children. A pause of 8 days seemed too long to us, so we sat down with the child after 4 days, and did so in such a way as to make the situation as identical as possible to that of the primary report.

Here we see how much difference age makes in determining how durable children's recollections are. Whereas the older children showed no degradation at all in the quality of the secondary reports they gave after 7 days in comparison to the primary report, there was a clear drop-off in Eva's case.

As in the first report, we again found that only four objects were named spontaneously, and among these was a person who was named incorrectly. The probing question about what else was in the picture sufficed to remind her of another person (Elsie, her nanny).

The questioning session then showed that she was still confusing the breakfast picture with the kitchen picture by Walters, but this confusion was an oscillating one, so that Eva was able to identify the mistakes resulting from it. At first she had the image of the woman with the soup spoon standing at the soup pot. Then this image was suppressed by another, correct one, whereby the woman was holding "*just bread.*" The two denials (of the mug and the knife) that had occurred in the primary questioning occurred again. Because of the influence of a leading question, something was now added: She believed that one could see "*nothing but little pots.*" The other four leading questions had no effect at all. [Table 8 summarizes the results of these experiments.]

## TESTIMONIES CONCERNING MATERIAL ENCOUNTERED REPEATEDLY

The second group of experiments that we conducted investigated the children's ability to recall material that had been more or less continuously present to them. These experiments were set up as follows.

## TABLE 8
### Breakfast Picture: Summary

| | | Hilde | | Günter | | | Eva | |
|---|---|---|---|---|---|---|---|---|
| | | **Total statements** | | | | | | |
| | | t | f | t | f | u | t | f |
| Primary | Report | 20 | 2 | 20 | 1 | — | 4 | — |
| | Question | 33 | 9 | 32 | 12.5 | 2 | 26 | 5 |
| Total | | 53 | 11 | 52 | 13.5 | 2 | 30 | 5 |
| Secondary | Report | 22 | 3 | 23 | 2 | — | 4 | 1 |
| | Question | 32 | 6 | 31 | 10 | — | 25 | 7 |
| Total | | 54 | 9 | 54 | 12 | — | 29 | 8 |
| | | **Statements concerning colors** | | | | | | |
| | | t | f | t | f | | t | f |
| Primary | Report | 4 | — | — | — | | — | — |
| | Question | 3 | 4 | 7 | 5.5 | | 0 | 2 |
| Total | | 7 | 4 | 7 | 5.5 | | 0 | 2 |
| Secondary | Report | 6 | 1 | — | — | | — | — |
| | Question | 4 | 2 | 9 | 4 | | 0 | 1 |
| Total | | 10 | 3 | 9 | 4 | | 0 | 1 |
| | | **Answers to leading questions** | | | | | | |
| | | t | f | t | f | | t | f |
| Primary | | 5 | 0 | 3 | 2 | | 5 | 0 |
| Secondary | | 4 | 0 | 3 | 1 | | 4 | 1 |
| | | **Spontaneity (ratio of correct statements in the report to all correct statements)** | | | | | | |
| Primary | | 38% | | 38.5% | | | 13% | |
| Secondary | | 41% | | 42% | | | 14% | |

Note: t = true; f = false; u = uncertain.

There has been a simple picture with vivid colors (a hung tapestry portraying "the shepherdess of the geese" [see Figure 2, p. 92]) hanging in a prominent position in our children's room for years.

Without warning (i.e., without allowing the children to look at the picture once more *ad hoc*), we took them to a different room and asked them to tell us what they knew about the picture.

The experiment was not conducted with the three children at the same time, but instead was conducted with Hilde half a year before the other two. The ages of the three children at the time of the experiment were 7;8, 6;0, and 3;6½. The picture had been visible to the children daily (except during travel) for 2½ to 3 years.

*Figure 2.*

As usual, the experiments consisted of a report and then a session of questioning according to a previously determined list of questions. This list also contained some questions requiring the children to estimate. But in this experiment, too, the great age difference between the children precluded rigid adherence to a prescribed procedure. Especially with the youngest child, it proved necessary to drop many questions that she could not understand, and to reformulate other questions in a way better suited to her age. So at first we present the report and the answers given during questioning for each child separately [Tables 9, 10 and 11]. We indicate erroneous statements by showing correct answers in brackets. At the end we present for comparative purposes the results in a summary table (Table 12). There, *t* signifies a correct statement, *f* a false statement, and *u* an uncertainty ("I don't know"). The questions (designed to induce the children to estimate) have been left out of the summary table and will be treated separately at the end.

7;8    There were no mistakes at all in the account of the picture given spontaneously by Hilde, but only once did she name a color, and it was a very obvious one (*green meadow*). When we tried to help her around this deficiency with the encouraging question "Do you know anything about the colors?" she at first gave a factual statement and then made two statements about colors, one of which was incorrect.

The questioning session yielded 15 correct and 5 incorrect elements (disregarding guesses). Among the errors, none resulted from Hilde having added something mistakenly. On the other hand, she denied two things (the head- and footwear of the shepherdess) that were in fact present. The remaining three mistakes had to do with colors (balanced by three correct statements about color).

With regard to guesses, because we had never allowed her to practice this task, the results were not all bad. The stated number of trees was exactly correct, and she only slightly overestimated how many pieces of fruit were on each tree, though she reported twice as many geese as there were.

## TABLE 9
### Picture of Geese: Hilde (7;8)

#### Report

*The shepherdess of the geese and just the geese. She's leading all of the geese. And just trees, pear trees or plumb trees. And a green meadow. The geese are quacking, many have their mouths open, their bills.* (Do you know anything about the colors?) *The geese are white. The maid had a white* [black] *apron.*

#### Questioning

| Mother | Hilde |
|---|---|
| Color of the trees? | *Green.* |
| What does one see on them? | *Curves.* |
| Their color? | *Blue.* [Yellow] |
| Do the trees have large trunks? | *No, short ones.* |
| Can all of them be seen entirely? | *No, one is cut off on the side.* |
| How are they arranged? | *Some toward the front, some behind.* |
| Where are more? | *Behind.* |
| The bills of the geese? | *Yellowish.* |
| Bodies? | *White.* |
| Feet? | *Brown.* |
| What does one see in the meadow? | *Flowers.* |
| Does one actually see them? | *Only white specks.* |
| How does the maid look? | *Round face.* |
| Skirt? | *Blue.* [Red] |
| Does she have a cap on? | *No.* |
| What does she have in her hand? | *A stick.* |
| Is it smooth? | *Yes, only a couple of twigs on it, I think.* |
| Does one see her from the front or side? | *From the side.* |
| Are the trees close together or spread out? | *Close together.* |
| Does the maid have shoes or is she barefoot? | *Barefoot.* [Wooden shoes] |
| Toward which side is she standing? | *Like this.* |
| About how many trees are there? | *5 or 6.* |
| About how many fruits in each tree? | *5.* |
| How many geese? | *12.* |

The spatial alignment of the elements in the picture was reported without error.

One statement (which happened to be correct) was qualified by the expression "*I think.*"

**6;0** Günter's report is quite different in that colors are mentioned spontaneously, twice correctly and once incorrectly. Otherwise, the report contains eight correct statements and one false one (he saw the shepherdess's staff as a rake).

During the questioning session he was more accurate than Hilde. One notices of these two children that the boy is more visual than his sister. For one thing, his six answers to questions about colors are all correct. Moreover he includes details that his sister perhaps never noticed. Most prominent in this regard is his statement that many of the geese have a bit of black at the tip of the tail. The strength of the visual sense in Günter's case was also clearly manifested in earlier recollections (cf. pp. 61 and 62).

The stated number of trees is approximately correct, the number of geese slightly overstated, and the stated number of fruit is about triple the actual number.

The four instances in which Günter states "*I think*" (he was, incidentally, correct in each case) show that he takes a self-critical position with respect to his own recollections. That these were not merely empty words but instead the genuine expression of an element of uncertainty can be seen in the fact that he uttered these words in connection with the red skirt both in the report and during questioning.

Günter looked at the picture by himself after the experiment and studied it closely. After some time, he was still bent over the picture, and he called to us: "*I know what I said wrong: The apron is not white but black; the trees stand somewhat apart from one another; the woman does not have a rake, and there are only six geese.*" With the exception of a trivial mistake (namely, that the trees were cut off on both sides of the picture) and the false estimate of the number of fruit, he found by himself all of the mistakes he had made. This ability to self-correct is surely connected to the previously mentioned ability to be self-critical. (See Table 10.)

**3;6½** To elicit a report from the 3½-year-old Eva we asked her: "Do you know what picture is hanging on the door of the children's room?" Answer: "*The geese.*" Thus assured that she had the correct picture in mind, we could ask her about the contents (see Table 11).

Her report is meager, containing four statements, one of which is false.

The questioning session yielded a report that was replete with errors. The number of correct and incorrect statements was about the same. Errors

## TABLE 10
### Picture of Geese: Günter (6;0)

**Report**

*Well the woman, she was walking, has a white [black] apron and a red skirt, I think. Green trees, with apples that are falling down and many geese. The woman has a rake [shepherdess's staff]; it was sort of a long pole.*

**Questioning**

| Mother | Günter |
|---|---|
| Color of the apples? | *Yellow.* |
| Do the trees have large trunks? | *No.* |
| How are they, then? | *There's not much to see.* |
| Can one see all of them? | *No: here* (points right) *at the edge of the tapestry a quarter is missing, and here also* (at the left) *another quarter is missing.* |
| Are there more in the back or in the front? | *In the back.* |
| Color of the geese's bills? | *Yellow.* |
| Bodies? | *White. On many of them, the tip of the tail has a little bit of black.* |
| Feet? | *Yellow, I think.* |
| What does one see in the meadow? | *Flowers, grass.* |
| Can one really see the flowers? | *No, they are just round specks.* |
| What does the shepherdess look like? | *White cap, white [black] apron and, I think, a red skirt.* |
| Does one see her from the front or the side? | *From the side.* |
| Are the trees close together or spread out? | *Very close together.* |
| Is the woman going barefoot or does she have shoes? | *I think she is wearing slippers.* |
| Toward which side is she facing? | *This way.* |
| About how many trees are there? | *6, 5, or 4.* |
| How many fruits in each tree? | *About 10.* |
| How many geese? | *8.* |

**Self-correction while looking at the picture**

*The apron is black.*
*The trees are spread out.*
*She does not have a rake.*
*There are 6 geese.*

## TABLE 11
## Picture of Geese: Eva (3;6½)

### Report

(Do you know what picture is hanging on the door to the children's room?) *The geese.*
(What is in the picture?) *A woman. And there are geese running around. The woman is feeding the geese.* [Incorrect]

### Questioning

| Mother | Eva |
|---|---|
| Are there trees? | *No, but there are some in the street.* [Incorrect] |
| Are there little apples? | *Yes, yellow apples.* |
| Are all of the geese running behind the woman? | *No.* |
| Are some running in front of her? | *Yes.* |
| What do their beaks look like? | *Red.* |
| And their bodies? | *White.* |
| Feet? | *Red.* |
| What can we see in the meadow? | *That is not a meadow.* [Incorrect] |
| What does the woman look like? | *White cap.* |
| Skirt? | *Blue.* [Red] |
| Apron? | *White.* [Black] |
| What does she have in her hand? | *Food for the geese.* [shepherdess's staff] |
| Do we see her from the front or the side? | *From the front.* [From the side] |
| Does she have shoes or is she barefoot? | *Shoes.* |
| How is the woman standing? | *Like I'm standing.* [She stands facing front] |

occurred especially in the area of colors (four out of seven were incorrect), even though the child has known the major colors well for 6 months.

The reason for the many errors is not really that the child has a bad memory, but rather that Eva is still not able to distinguish which of the many vivid memoric images she has belongs to which of her many different experiences. On this occasion, too, there were confusions between this picture and others—for example, a picture hanging in the children's bedroom, in which a woman is facing forward and feeding fowls. Moreover, a well-known psychological effect is seen, whereby the possible becomes reality: the skirt could be blue, the apron could be white, and the 3½-year-old child is still not critical enough of herself to be able to say such things as "I think" or "I don't know."

Eva's ability to withstand suggestions, mentioned earlier (see p. 90) was apparent again in this instance. The question carrying with it a precondition—"What do we see in the meadow?"—was rejected: *"That's not a meadow."* Because she apparently had never seen the green background as a meadow, she was not going to be influenced in this regard even by such a pointed question. The contradiction originated in the fact that the child had indeed seen the apples but not the trees results from the peculiar stylization of the trees. Our experience has been that even adults can have difficulty recognizing them.

We did not ask Eva questions that would require her to estimate, because she still does not have a firm grasp of numerosity even though she can name the numbers up to 20.

## SUMMARY

If one compares the three children in both series of experiments, it is evident that in each instance the two older children are relatively close to one another, whereas Eva is separated from them by a considerable distance (see Table 12). Perhaps we have a result with general validity: With respect to the ability to testify, the distance between the 3-year-old and the 5-year-old seems to be more pronounced than that between the 5- and 7-year-old.

On closer analysis, one sees that the deficit of the 3-year-old is relatively minimal when the testimony is given directly after close study of the

TABLE 12
Picture of Geese: Summary

| | Hilde | | Günter | | Eva | |
|---|---|---|---|---|---|---|
| | *All statements* | | | | | |
| | *t* | *f* | *t* | *f* | *t* | *f* |
| Report | 10 | 1 | 10 | 2 | 3 | 1 |
| Questioning | 15 | 5 | 20 | 2 | 7 | 6 |
| Total | 25 | 6 | 30 | 4 | 10 | 7 |
| | *Statements concerning color* | | | | | |
| | *t* | *f* | *t* | *f* | *t* | *f* |
| Report | 2 | 1 | 2 | 1 | 0 | 0 |
| Questioning | 3 | 3 | 6 | 0 | 3 | 4 |
| Total | 5 | 4 | 8 | 1 | 3 | 4 |

object (Breakfast picture, primary report). To be sure, the 3-year-old's knowledge is much more impoverished than that of her siblings (30 correct statements versus more than 50), but the number of errors is also relatively small. The major difference lies in the degree of "spontaneity": Of all the things she remembered, the youngest child included on her own only 13% in her original report. The great majority was not reported until she was prompted by questioning. In the cases of the two older children, spontaneity was about three times as great (38%).

When the conditions for giving the testimony became more difficult, the gap between Eva and her siblings widened immediately.

One problem was the passing of a several-day interval (Breakfast picture, secondary report). Although the older children, remarkably, were more accurate after the 8-day pause than they had been previously, Eva showed an increase in the number of errors (from five to eight) despite the fact that the interval lasted only 5 days.

The picture of the geese presented a second complication in that attention was not focused exclusively on studying the picture, so that the children's testimony had to be based on an adventitiously formed impression of their room. In the case of the little one, the number of correctly remembered elements equaled only one third or two fifths, respectively, of the elements correctly remembered by Günter and Hilde (10 versus 30 and 10 versus 25, respectively). In spite of this, the number of errors was not only relatively but also absolutely higher in Eva's case.

This result—one that at present pertains to just one individual—can be formulated as follows: Under especially favorable conditions, the 3-year-old child delivers testimony to which we may attach a certain plausibility. But every complication of the conditions of testimony reduces its value to a much greater extent than is the case with older children. A replication of these results, possibly in a kindergarten or even in home studies, would be an important contribution, and not only for theoretical reasons.

The substantial convergence in the performances of the two older children (refer to the tables) might seem surprising at first, but it would be a mistake to generalize these results either across age or gender. Certainly there is no moratorium between the ages of 5 and 7 in the development of the ability to testify, nor should the comparability of Günter's performance with that of his older sister be taken as evidence that, in general, boys have some sort of an advantage over girls. We believe we are simply dealing with an individual difference between Günter and Hilde. Günter's strong visual sense, especially his perception of colors, had such a powerful effect that it overcompensated for his deficiency—in comparison to his sister—with respect to suggestibility. Evidence of this comes from the study involving the often-seen picture of the geese, where he not only equaled but surpassed his sister (30 versus 25 correct statements; 4 versus 6 false statements). In this case, where it was not a matter of a one-time concentration of attention but rather of a habitual and recurrent exposure, conditions were especially favorable for his natural inclination toward the visual and his great interest in images.

Finally, it also bears mentioning that the results obtained with Hilde and Günter in the case of the secondary report (Breakfast picture) revealed no negative effects of the 8-day pause. If anything, they showed the opposite. (The number of errors in Hilde's case dropped from 11 to 9, and in Günter's case from $13\frac{1}{2}$ to 12.) In any case, these results indicate that, at least over limited time intervals, there can be exceptions to the well-known dependence of memory on time. Other researchers have already reported similar findings [see, e.g., Jaffa, 1903; Diehl, 1903; Lobsien, 1903, 1905].

# 9

# FALSIFICATION OF TESTIMONY THROUGH FANTASY

Mistaken recollections involve complete belief in their correctness. At this point, however, we move into a middle territory where testimony oscillates back and forth between appearance and reality as a result of the playful activity of fantasy. In these instances, the degree to which the child is conscious of the illusion can vary widely.

For an adult there is only one reality that can be accorded the status of truth. In this reality, everything is related to and accommodates everything else, and brought into logical, causal, and teleological coherence. What is not included is not real: It is either appearance or deception. For the child, things are different. At 3 years of age, the child is still living in the momentary present. But within this present, the child is able to separate play and reality by means of clear sensory experiences, so that in this instance, seriously intended correct testimonies are still often possible.[27] In contrast, the child becomes seriously aware of the not-present only gradually and with difficulty. The child still does not build firm bridges forward into the future, and even less so into the past. Even when thought exceeds very limited time durations, the child still lacks insight into the criterion of true objectivity: that everything that really happens both is a consequence and has consequences. Hence the child often enough does not distinguish sharply between the seriousness of reality and that which is whimsical, imaginative, or based on fantasy.

Earlier (see p. 34), we commented on this peculiar mixture of appearance and reality, of play and seriousness. At this point we can provide additional examples of this.

Very early on, we noticed our son's active imagination. There was a period (2;9 until 3;0, shortly after the birth of his younger sister) during which, often for hours at a time during the day, he would take on other roles and would often assign other roles to others. "He calls himself the 'ohdda sissa,' and gives his real big sister various other names: 'lil'sissa,' 'Kitty,' or 'Gettud' (Gertrude); mother is 'bigmother.' Many days he is 'Muttsen' (little mother) and looks after his 'little' (in reality older) sister. What is peculiar about this is that he also injects these imaginations into situations of reality—for example, at lunch time or when getting dressed, and he is quite beside himself when someone tries to correct him by using the correct names. He even calls himself 'ohdda sissa' when among strangers, and even carries the self-deception over in situations of strong affective arousal."

**2;10** "When crying and greatly agitated, even in the middle of the night, he does not let go of his fantasy. One recent evening I heard him crying hard in bed, and when I asked him what was wrong, he cried inconsolably that he had lost his little ball and his big ball in the alley. He implored me: '*Tomorrow bigmother and ohdda sissa should go to find the balls, and the little kitty should not come along.*' He was so sad that it was even fruitless to console him by saying that I would buy him a new ball: '*No, don't buy a ball, find the big and the little ball,*' he moaned—and this underscores the point that he did not deviate from the roles he had assigned to himself, older sister, and mother." This infusion of illusion into affect parallels the story of Hilde and the bears mentioned on page 35.

**3;5** We have a corresponding example from our daughter Eva. Mother reports, "We talked about Hilde's sewing basket, and Eva said playfully: '*I have a sewing basket, too; I got it as a gift from grandmother.*' Hilde and Günter acted very surprised, and I said, 'Oh, Eva is just kidding.' Then Eva said, '*No, really I have gotten one from grandmother.*' To which her brother replied indignantly, '*That's a lie, Eva.*' Out of consideration for the older siblings, who already distinguish rigorously between truth and lie, I could not let the matter drop there. I asked Eva to go fetch the sewing box. At this she became quite sullen, and fought back tears, but it took her quite a long time before she finally decided to respond to our repeated question about whether she had really received a sewing box by saying '*no.*'" Perhaps many events of this sort could be classified as lies, but the written record of what literally has been said in some given instance is not adequate for purposes of learning how to evaluate a psychological process in which proper interpretation requires one to take into account the entire context of the developmental sequence. Here, all accompanying nuances (expression, mimic, etc.) can play an important role as well.[28]

Once with Eva we were able to investigate one of those stories that are told in full awareness of their fabrication. We did this by making a stenographic recording as she went along. This story is different from the telling of a fairy tale in that the child organizes the fantasied production around her own self, and in this way is able to lend to the production a touch of reality:

3;5   Eva was with her mother in the kitchen; and just as mother was ready to tell Eva a story, Eva broke in: "*Should I tell you a story about a little baby?*—*The little baby pecked a hole, with an umbrella she pecked a hole. When she opened up the umbrella, she poked herself in the head. So I went out quickly and got a bandage. Father gave me a large bandage, and I ripped it open* (by way of clarification: Eva is saying "I" meaning herself in the role of mother)—*and licked it and stuck it on the baby's head: and when it came off I put a new one on. But that made the little baby cry.*" (Compare Hilde's story about the dolls at exactly the same age, p. 34.)

In the literature, fantasies of this sort among schoolchildren have been reported regularly, but such material in the case of younger children is very rare.

With his son, Lindner [1898, p. 77] found the "desire to fabricate" very pronounced at the age of 2;6, whereas in the case of his daughter he did not observe anything of the kind. Lindner is correct to see these statements as forms of play rather than as lies. However, his explanation is inadequate from a psychological standpoint. According to him, no fantasy has "any goal other than to practice and use newly learned words." Moreover, there is no way that we should call it a fantastic "exaggeration" when the boy says seriously: "*Once a man shoots me* (= once a man shot me), or when he relates absolutely laughable things, the untruth of which is obvious even to the boy himself.

Karl Groos [1908, p. 189] reported that a 3½-year-old boy "was a great confabulator." [29] "He said he saw a fish in 'north Berlin' that looked like a shark and had feet with boots on. He also said once: 'In north Berlin there are rabbits and dogs on the roof. They climb up there with a little ladder and play around with one another up there . . . and then . . . and then there is a telephone, you know, with a long wire, and then on the wire they walk to Stuttgart.'"

Meumann [1907, p. 248] provides a parallel to Eva's story about the sewing box. He "knew a 4-year-old girl who related nonchalantly the experiences of her older, 6-year-old brother as if they had happened to her, even though the child had been raised in an exemplary fashion and was continuously corrected by her brother. For the girl, fantasy and recollection were continuously and uncritically intertwined with and confused with one another."

In his monograph dealing primarily with lying among older children, the Frenchman Duprat [1903, p. 60] also cites cases that are relevant. Note, however, that these findings were obtained in a government-sponsored survey [rather than in a scientifically designed investigation] and should therefore be viewed with great caution:

5;0 Duprat reports of a boy who, by listening to true stories, was prompted to make up untrue stories out of thin air. "And when one confronts him with his lies, he answers just as all impulsive people would and most people with active imaginations: 'It is not my fault, it is stronger than I am.'" Everyone who deals with children knows that would hardly be possible for a 5-year-old to give such an answer. Some further examples have to do with children ranging in age from $2\frac{1}{2}$ to 4 years, and these incline Duprat toward the conclusion: "A large number of young children have such lively fantasies that they playfully move into innocent lies" ("*se jouer dans des mensonges inoffensives*").

# 10

## PSEUDO-LIES AND LIES

The falsifications of testimony that we have considered thus far—actual recollective deceptions as well as fantasized illusions in relating something—were impartial in nature in the sense that they had no bearing on any actual advantage or disadvantage to the child. In contrast to these are those false testimonies that have a direct bearing on the child's well-being or pain. Here we must look for psychological causes not in the child's ideational life (memory or fantasy) but rather in the functions of affect and will.

With this we encounter another polarity: Although the vast majority of impartial falsifications of testimony has a positive content (i.e., the falsifications involve imagining something that is not actually there), almost all of the child's self-serving falsifications entail denial. Many—most of the relatively harmless ones—end with the negation, appearing as untruthful defense, rejection, or denial. Others go further, from spoken and unspoken denial to positive falsifications—for example, to blaming others, excuse-making, feigning of pain, and so forth.

These self-serving falsifications of testimony, which occur with all children, need not always be genuine lies, but they do form a transition to genuine lies, and whether the seed of lying subsequently dies out or develops in a given child depends on both inner and outer factors—in other words, on inner dispositions and on child-rearing practices.

This chapter will follow the sequence of stages to its end in fully formed lies.

# DEFENSE

Defending against what is unpleasant is part of human survival. In the case of the child, its predominantly affective–volitional nature leads to the use of this defense in a wide variety of forms: Language serves this purpose as well as gesticulation and mimic. The linguistic means by which a mature person can deny or doubt certain facts are more often used by children to defend against unpleasantness without actually intending to lie. If we say something to the child that is embarrassing to him or her, she or he has need for words of defense regardless of whether the embarrassing remark relates to the future, the present, or the past. In the latter two cases, we have the appearance of a lie. The point mentioned on p. 33, where Hilde said "*no*" in defense against being reminded of something embarrassing to her, is relevant. Other children provide evidence that pertains as well.[30]

**2;10½** Once, in a temper, Günter threw a punch at his father. Father asked, "What did you just do?" Günter: "*I don't know.*" Father persisted earnestly but in a friendly way, and when instead of resorting to words of defense Günter tried to run away, father dragged him back and said again: "What did you do?" Günter (ashamedly): "*Hit.*"

**1;9** Ament [1899, p. 94] reports of his niece that she had received slaps on the hand from her mother in the morning. In the evening, when she was asked in her father's presence: "Did you get slaps on the hand today?" she said "*No,*" and Ament viewed this denial as "the first lie." The interpretation seems erroneous to us. The child had learned the word "*no*" only 14 days previously, and our observations suggest to us that a considerable time must pass before the *no* that is originally used in a purely affective way can be understood or used at all in a way that expresses a declaration of meaning [Stern & Stern, 1907].

Other ways of speaking that make substantive sense to us can also be understood by the child as forms of affective defense, and used as such. For example, Günter used the special construction: "*No, 'spensive!*" ("No, that is too expensive!") to convey the general meaning: "That does not suit me," or "I'm not interested in that." [Stern & Stern, 1907]. We had often used those words to deny him wishes having to do with purchasing attractive things. But he had understood the expression only as a defense and not as reason, and so he used it when he was being taken to bed, or when someone disturbed him while he was playing and so forth.

Although in this case the unusual expression of defense seems comical to adults, the same sort of use in other analogous cases can create the impression of lying. Included would be those instances, repeatedly mentioned in the literature, of simulating pain to avoid something unpleasant.

At first these words might give expressions to genuine pain. The child then associates the same sounds with success in getting help or comfort. Then, consistent with the change of meaning that occurs so regularly at this age, the success brought by the expressions becomes prominent and the specific occasions for their use recedes into the background. Thus there can be cases in which the words being used are no longer expressive (i.e., indicating displeasure or discomfort) but purely teleological (i.e., striving toward something desired). In line with these notions, it appears to us, contrary to Ament [1899, p. 82], that the following case does not actually involve a lie: A girl aged 1;9 and suffering from chicken pox had said "ow!" with each painful touch, and in response to that had been left alone. Subsequently, she responded resentfully "no ow" when she was busily preoccupied with her own game and did not want to be bothered. This "ow" has the same symbolic function as Günter's "No, 'spensive!" It is not a pretense of a reason for defense: It is defense pure and simple. Presumably, the same interpretation is to be given for what little Hans Lipmann said.

2;0   "Mama. Pail heavy." The pail was not heavy at all, but for the boy it was burdensome, and so he used this form of complaint in an attempt to transfer the burden to his mother.

Who would claim that a 6-month-old baby could "lie"? And yet lying there dry and satiated, the child who has previously experienced that if she cries "waa waa" when hungry, wet, or in pain, then some friendly being helps or changes the situation, cries again not because those conditions exist again but because she seeks to gain the attention of that friendly being. Often enough the concerned mother will, on the basis of a false interpretation, respond to the original motives of the crying under circumstances in which only wishes associated with those motives (e.g., gaining attention) are at play. Yet the same altered meaning that is entailed by the "waa waa" cry of the 6-month-old child is present in the case of the "ow" of the 2-year-old, or in other similar instances in which words originally used to express pain are now being used differently. These latter cases (with older children) are subject to the same false interpretations as are the former cases (involving infants).

Entirely analogous to these are cases in which 1- to 2-year-old children appear to be faking a need to be taken out of bed, or the wagon, or a chair, and so forth. Again, experience has taught them that those expressions of need always succeed in producing the desired change. At this point, it is not necessary for the child to really have to go to the bathroom, because the other associations are now strong enough by themselves to call forth the expression. Preyer [1905] and Schäfer [1905, p. 198] give examples of this from the middle of the second year, and Oltuscewski gives an example from the 12th month.

Apart from these typical occurrences there are special situations that can result in the child being misunderstood. Only rarely are these kinds of cases pursued to their true sources with the kind of psychological empathy displayed by Schäfer [1905, p. 200] who reports the following of his 2-year-old son.

**2;0** The child had broken a plate. In response to the pointed questioning of his mother about who had done that, the child at first answered, ashamed, "*Beddy*" (= I want to go to bed) and when mother asked again, the child said "*Papa*." Schäfer does not interpret this response as confirmation of a lie in the sense of meaning "Papa did it." Instead, and consistent with the overall relationship between father and son, Schäfer sees this as the child's expression of the wish to flee to his father and away from the punishment he expects to receive from mother. In fact, an event that happened soon thereafter confirmed this view. The child had splashed water out on the balcony and gotten himself dirty. When mother came to him with a stern look on her face, the child called out eagerly, as if to divert his mother's attention to something else, "*Go for a ride!*" In response to mother's stern admonition, "You should not get yourself dirty!" the child said "*Papa*." Viewed in its proper context, this "*Papa*" was understood only as a wish on the child's part to escape his increasingly angry mother and flee to father.

One can only agree with this interpretation. The child does not really answer the question actually asked. He attends only to the threat, and seeks to escape what seems to be in store—at first by wishing to be taken to bed or taken for a ride, and later by wanting to flee to father. That the word "*Papa*" can be misinterpreted as an answer to the question—and hence a false assertion—is a consequence of the immaturity of the child who is 2 years old. Laconically, the child uses one and the same word in quite different senses.

Up to the end of the 2nd year of life, most so-called lies are the result of false interpretations on the part of adults, and these must be avoided all the more in instances in which they can have pedagogical consequences of fateful influence on the child's later fidelity to the truth. But we discuss this further in a separate chapter.

If false assertions made for purely defensive reasons really are not lies at all, we move now into that transitional area in which there are many more psychological and pedagogical difficulties.

Even the 3- to 5-year-old child still has the initial tendency to defend against the unpleasant in situations in which he or she fears the consequences, and indeed most often (as with the younger child) with words of denial. But these primary reactions are no longer the only ones, because with increasing insight the (somewhat older) child now begins to actively take positions. As a consequence, the child now comes to sense more or less clearly the contradiction between his or her words and reality. With this insight, the child normally has the strength of will not to allow the defense to stand as a denial but instead to express the truth about matters.

The adult experiences this process in a similar way, but unlike the child is able to inwardly overcome the first inclination—namely, the wish to escape what is embarrassing or troublesome. Not so with the immature person. The child projects outwardly what is transpiring within, and only after defending him- or herself in this way is the child amenable to correction or self-correction. It therefore depends in large part on the caregivers whether this tendency to take back false assertions develops as it should or is instead choked off in its early stages and replaced by a tendency to lie out of fear. Several examples may serve to clarify what is meant.

**3;4½** His mother writes of Günter: "I noticed that a piece of wallpaper was hanging torn on the wall. The stool that was standing there was positioned as Günter was accustomed to placing it while playing, so that the perpetrator was unmistakably him. I asked Hilde and Günter: 'Who tore the piece of wallpaper?' Hilde answered in a confident tone: 'Not I.' Günter remained facing in the opposite direction and said likewise: 'Not I.' Calmly, I said to him: 'Come here.' Günter put his hands behind his back: '*But don't paddle.*' That in itself was an admission, because he had never been paddled when he did not deserve it. I: '*No, I won't paddle you. Now come, my boy. Look here: did you tear that?*' Günter: '*Yes.*' I perceived the opportunity to make clear to him that good children always speak the truth immediately." The fear of a punishment, even a small one, led Günter at first to defensive utterances ("*Not I*" and "*But don't paddle.*") But when he noticed that there was nothing to fear, he calmly replaced his defensive utterances with the truth. With such young children, whose firm character is yet to be formed, it is necessary above all to make it easy for them to overcome the tendency toward defensive utterances. At this age, it should not be demanded of a child that he succeed in overcoming his initial defensive tendency completely on his own, without support.

**3;4½** Three months later, Günter behaved in a very similar way when he had strewn little strips of cardboard around his room. His mother, on entering the room, asked: "Who did this?" Again, Günter called out as did Hilde: "*Not I.*" Patiently, mother repeated the question, and Günter said: "*I did.*" Here was an instance of self-correction, without need of a calming assurance that there would be no punishment.

Although still in his 5th year we find the boy making occasional although rare attempts to deny things, the denial always yields to the first admonishing question. In his case, none of these instances led to an out-and-out lie, and in his 6th year he became, to the contrary, something of a truth fanatic. This will be discussed further later on.

**3;2**  Our daughter Eva occasionally offers us little momentary untruths, that, however, quickly play themselves out harmlessly when handled appropriately. Mother writes: "A pretense, more precisely a fake cough. . . . Because Eva had a cold, we had suspended our usual evening cold bath, something that continued to be unpleasant for her anyway. One day I said: 'We can start the cold baths again now.' At this our sly little daughter Eva said, 'Oh, no, I still have a cough,' and she coughed in such a comical way that it was difficult to keep a straight face. I interposed, however: 'Eva, you don't have a cough. You must not say that, because it is not true.' It was clear to me that she understood me completely: the lower lip protruded further and further, she was about to cry, and it was obvious that she felt guilty. She submitted to the cold bath without making a sound."

**2;11¾**  A case reported by the Scupins [1907, p. 205] offers an illustration relevant to all that has been said to this point: "The boy came in today with a piece of mortar and said, half mischievously and half embarrassed, that it had broken off from the balcony. When he saw that a serious look suddenly came over our faces, he corrected himself quickly: 'No, no; a little bird broke it off.' When his parents went out and inspected the damage, they asked in a friendly way: 'Who's the naughty little bird that caused this damage?' The boy studied his parents' faces for a long time, and when he could discern in them nothing more of anger and seriousness, he said, swinging his arms in embarrassment, 'Oh, alright, it was me.'" True to his character, the boy reported spontaneously and in all innocence what he had done, then resorted to a defensive claim when he perceived a threat, but in turn quickly abandoned this again when he noticed that the parents were behaving in a friendly way.


## HARMLESS BLAMING

More ponderous than those false claims considered up to now, which serve only to negate (e.g., deny responsibility for something) are those that positively blame others. But even in this instance, there can be great psychological and moral differences buried beneath one and the same surface appearance.

There is an entirely harmless form of blaming for which the following cases may serve as examples.

**1;11**  At age 1;11 our Eva blamed everything that went wrong on Günter. She had so often heard her brother named as the perpetrator of various little accidents that in similar cases she simply conjured up the image of her brother in a purely associative way, and used the stereotyped formulation: "*Günter broke it.*" This case is unambiguous because Eva herself had not been involved in any of the incidents in question, was not even suspected, and so had no difficulties of her own to try to escape.

**3;6**  Of the same child, Mother reports something similar 1½ years later: "Eva found her hiking stick broken, lying near the cook. So who else could have broken it in two? She complained to me: '*Toni broke my stick.*' This was not true, and I asked Eva seriously: 'Did you see Toni break your stick?' Ashamed, she said '*no*'; and I warned her to say only what she had really seen. Promptly thereafter, the positive effect of this warning manifested itself. When the nanny arrived, Eva said to her: '*Look, Else, my stick got broken all by itself.*' "

**2;11**  Günter, too, once blamed his sister when we asked, "Who tore the pages out of the book?" In all probability, he had not done it, but in any case he was convinced of his innocence. So the question must have been a leading one and must have logically pointed to the only other person who could have been considered a possible perpetrator (i.e., Eva). It is certainly well-known that leading questions are much more likely to elicit a positive answer than a negative one, and one can only speculate on how much damage has been done in children's playrooms by the leading question: "Who did that?"

**2;8**  The Scupins [1907, p. 156] report an especially instructive example of this in the case of their son. "He loves to pull keys from doors. But today, when he was asked about a missing key, he pondered the matter carefully at first, and then said, '*Ask Sohni*' (a playmate). But Sohni did not know anything about the key, and when we went back to the boy with our original question, he thought some more and said with conviction: '*The spider ate up the key* (regarding this spider, see the subsequent section on pedagogy). 'Bubi, that is not true.' '*Oh, a dog came and chewed the key off.*' 'That's not true, either, Bubi.' '*But aunt Martha took the key and went into the stairwell.*' Later we learned that in fact the boy had had nothing to do with the disappearance of the key but had given his answers partly because there was a demand for an explanation and partly because of the leading nature of the questions."

In the next section, we turn to a discussion of blaming that cannot be considered harmless.


## THE GENUINE LIE

As the previous discussion shows, many—indeed most—of the so-called lies of early childhood are not immoral in the way that they might seem to be. They are either mistaken claims made in good faith or momentary, impulsive utterances that signify nothing beyond themselves. In contrast to these there are genuine lies—that is, consciously false assertions in which a purposive and deliberate attempt is made to deceive others. We should not preclude the possibility that such deliberate lies occur even in early childhood. They might occur only occasionally with some children, more regularly with others, and in a few cases—always as a consequence of abnormal psychological or rearing conditions—habitually.

The serious attempt to give the appearance of truth to something that is false can be executed through persistence, or through deliberation, or through a combination of both. Of course, persistence cannot be expressed in absolute time intervals. Persistence in a lie can be established with a few minutes if within this time interval all warning and questioning remains fruitless. On the other hand, a lie does not have to be regarded as "persistent" even if a half an hour passes between its expression and its admission. Deliberation can precede a lie or accompany it. It extends not only to the planning of the lie itself and to such consequences as the lie will entail when questioning begins but sometimes also to actual activities intended to make the falsified content of the lie seem as plausible as possible. Persistence alone accompanies a negative lie, which serves only the function of denying a happening or doing. Deliberation must occur in the case of a positive lie, and this can extend from mere excuse-making to the deceitful blaming of others.

From the material we have gathered thus far based on our observations of our own children, we have not been able to confirm any instance of a genuine lie. On this topic, therefore, we must turn to the literature and to some privately obtained communications.

Scupin's diary supplied several examples, and it is interesting to see how even when the child is too young to speak, deceitfulness and attempts to deceive already anticipate later real lies. Incidentally, such instances occur only occasionally in the case of Scupin's boy, and, as with most children, one usually finds him to be naively open in the confession of his little sins.

The first example of a deliberate deception was observed before the end of the first year [1907, p. 49]. The boy liked to tear up paper, and while doing this was in the habit of taking the last little bit of paper and putting it into his mouth. Despite his having been forbidden to do this, he would persist in the activity once he had determined that he was not being watched. "Today the child's mother suddenly turned toward him and caught him chewing paper. Frightened, he flinched, took the paper out of his mouth, and laughed in embarrassment at his mother to make a joke of the incident. But his mother remained serious, repeated that eating paper was forbidden, and then pointedly turned her back on the child. The boy giggled to himself, cast a furtive glance and was slyly sidling over to his mother, intending to let the paper disappear into his mouth when his mother quickly turned around. Startled, he blinked and gave out a short, muffled laugh of embarrassment—so that he could suddenly and with the most innocent looking expression lay the scrap of paper on his nose, his eyes and his ear, as if he had intended to do this all along and had only accidentally brought the paper close to his mouth."

**1;10** Ten months later his mother writes [1907, p. 89]: "As soon as one leaves the room or appears to be asleep, he gets into all sorts of mischief. Furtively, he checks the door, or he makes sure that the person sleeping really has his or her eyes closed. If he senses that he has been caught, he shows his guilt immediately. He blushes easily, brings the [forbidden] object to us, laughing nervously, and surrenders it with a '*Thank you.*'—Today his father heard the child in the adjoining room handling a glass. He called out 'Bubi.' No answer. Usually, the boy comes quickly and happily, but this time he was worried about the glass. Raising his voice, his father now ordered, 'Bring the glass here immediately.' '*No,*' contradicted the boy, but very quietly. The order was repeated more pointedly, and the boy finally came hurrying with a wooden toy: '*There.*' Clearly, he wanted to make his father think that he had been playing with the wooden toy and not with the forbidden glass. This was the first bad act of dishonesty that the boy committed. The glass was standing on the stool, and in response to yet another and very ominous warning, the child delivered it unwillingly." Here we have in fact all of the defining characteristics of a genuine lie: The deception is carried out consciously, persistently, and deliberately with the goal of escaping punishment.

If in this case, as usually, the lie occurred as a direct reaction to outer influences, the following cases involving the same boy are of interest because they entail spontaneity. In each of these cases, an attempt was made to avoid blame or punishment by making a false statement before being asked about the matter in question.

**2;5½** "In a rare occurrence, he tried to conceal something. He called to mother from the bed: '*Bubi was a good boy, had a good nap. Bubi didn't wet his diaper . . . Bubi was a good boy.*' This exaggerated self-praise and the boy's wide-eyed anxious look seemed suspicious to the mother, and her suspicion was justified" [1907, p. 139].

**2;9** "He tried very hard to remove a wooden fastening that was attached to a box to secure it, and as he succeeded in this, he brought it to us saying: '*This broke by itself.*' He said this with a half-sly and half-guilty looking expression, and really was not quite sure what reaction he was going to get to what he had done" [1907, p. 165].

We also have private communications from Mrs. Lipmann concerning observations made around the same time of early childhood, which are similar to the Scupin cases.

1;3½ "Hans wanted to put his thumb into his mouth. His father reprimanded him and said, 'Hey!' At which Hans suddenly acted quite innocently and waved to his father as if he had never had the intention of sucking his thumb."

1;5½ "Hans reacts wonderfully to glances. When he does something he is not supposed to do, I look at him in a certain way and he understands immediately, but then often acts as if he had intended to do something else all along."

The following reports concerning somewhat older children were made available to us privately. The little girl X did not begin to tell untruths until she was in her 4th year. Her mother assures us that prior to that time she had not noticed any such attempts.

3;4 Once, she was eating soup alone in her little bed. To be more precise, she was not eating the soup but instead splashing around in it with her hands, as if she were washing herself. Her mother came and noticed how, right away, the child pulled her hands back. Her mother asked, "What were you doing?" Answer: "*Nothing*." Mother pressed her, but the stubborn child did not answer any more. Not until several minutes later did she admit her guilt in response to the mother's questioning.

4;9 The girl Y had the bad habit of biting her nails and picking her nose. When the child was 4¾ years old, she often denied having done these forbidden things, even when there was clear evidence to the contrary. It was only after the parents had persisted for a long time that Y admitted her guilt. Once she denied vehemently that she had bitten her fingernails, and when she was told to show her hands, she clenched them tightly together and would not open them up despite repeated warnings. She was then struck firmly on her fingers, and finally opened them up, and in the face of the clear evidence that she had bitten her fingernails she admitted it.

Marcinowsky [1905, p. 203] places emphasis on a special category of children's lies—specifically, the appeal to some hindering circumstance or other (pains, satiation, fatigue, etc.) to escape an undesired situation. Marcinowski does not regard these as harmless attempts by the children to excuse themselves[31] and he even says that he thinks the unconscious lying that is entailed by such excuse-making is the rule among children. Marcinowski reports the following of his daughter (whose age, though not given precisely, was certainly less than 4 years): "She gets stomachaches with lawlike regularity whenever we are eating rice dishes, but with equal regularity does not get any such pains when we are having chocolate, pudding, or similar things, even though these things usually cause her to have diarrhea and colic." This case certainly involves a lie resulting from the disinclination toward rice dishes. However, the claim that such behavior is the rule among children is something that we must contest on the basis of our own observations as well as the observations of others that have been made available to us. With our children, too, it occurred, though only very rarely, that there was something that did not taste good to them. However, they never pretended to have any sort of pain but instead simply stuck with the truth of the matter.

One case that is far more serious than the others is the following one. It concerns a 4½ year-old girl, Z, who had to endure an especially strict and, in our view, unpedagogical upbringing by a nervous mother. As a result, this girl was highly anxious. Once when the mother was traveling, a woman stayed with the child, and it is to that woman that we owe thanks for this information.

**4;6**  Once, when Z found herself alone in the kitchen, she broke a glass. She was observed as she secretively hid the broken pieces in the oven and then went out. After some time, the kitchen staff arrived. Z followed them, pulled the broken pieces of glass out of the oven and asked, "*Now which of you did this?*" The helpers said to her face that she had done it. She contested that and even claimed that she had seen the helper who had broken the glass. It was only with the lengthy coaching of the woman who was caring for the child that the child admitted the lie and became very ashamed of herself.

At around the same age, Z. was once alone with her little sister in the room, and tried to squirt a liquid from a perfume bottle into the little one's mouth. In response to the loud cries of the little one, an adult hurried to the scene and asked what was happening. The little one said immediately: "*Squirting in mouth.*" Z. denied this and continued to deny it even after she was made to stand in the corner. Not until she was promised a sweet did she finally admit to what she had done. Whether at the time Z. was still a psychologically normal young girl is doubtful. In any case, we know that now, as a 12-year-old, she is seriously hysteric. However, the deceitfulness has given way to its opposite, a quite peculiar openness.

We will only mention that among children with pronounced pathologies lying can occur at an early age even in a serious form and with great regularity. Marcinowski supplies an example from a 3-year-old hysteric. Further literature concerning pathological lying in childhood can be found in Delbrück [1891], Piper [1906], and others.

# FANATICAL TRUTHFULNESS

The consideration of lies alone can never guarantee a correct picture of the attitude of the child toward truth and untruth. One must also observe the role played by the opposite behavior—namely, spontaneous truthfulness.

The young child normally expresses most of his or her inner experiences, and so it is much more natural for the child to naively and openly relate all experiences instead of keeping them to him- or herself or creating pretenses. This openness even extends to little mishaps, if strict demands being imposed by the caregiver have not at a very young age already disturbed the natural trust that would exist between that person and the child.

**2;5** Preyer [1905, p. 237] reports of his son that "the slightest wrong, the most insignificant misstep was immediately related by the child himself in a little report that he would make with characteristically naive seriousness." With Scupin's boy matters were much the same [1907, p. 146]: "The boy retells his little sins with a naive openness. For example, when we go into his room, we are met with his muffled voice: '*Bubi took some sugar*' or '*I ripped up paper again.*' Naturally, the punishment is rather mild in the face of such open admissions."

Beyond this, for comparative purposes one can consider corresponding behavior on the part of Hilde (pp. 31–32) and some cases reported by Compayre [1900, pp. 387–388].

**2;6** A still higher developmental level relevant to the present considerations is exemplified by an instance in which we noted of our daughter Eva—likewise at this young age.

"We showed Eva some flowers that her little brother had picked. At this, Eva (who liked to do, and to have done, everything that her siblings did and had done) said, '*I picked—I have sometimes picked—flowers, too.*' It occurred to her in the middle of her sentence that she had to correct herself to keep within the limits of the truth. So she already felt that without this modification her utterance would not have corresponded to the facts."

At a somewhat older age, then, this openness can develop into a moral quality, sometimes even into a pronounced truth fanaticism. This remains within the limits of normality as long as it leads to an insight, not entirely clear initially, into the ugliness of lying. In this instance the caregivers must handle matters deftly, so that a behavior that in its essence is so good does not become exaggerated into a sickness.[32] Temporary fanaticism of this sort is something we have observed from the 5th year of life on.

**5;4** In Günter's case we have some characteristic examples of this. Mother reports the following: "At the moment Günter is so cautious that he often follows up his statements by saying '. . . *at least I think so*.' Any sort of statement not entirely correct but said in good faith can bother him later on. For example, he had told his uncle that he owned two pencil cases with colored pencils. However, the one case contained not colored pencils but crayons without wood casing. In the evening he called me back to his bedside in the darkened room. He had remembered the conversation with his uncle and he scolded himself for the incorrectness of what he had said: that he really did not have two pencil cases but only one; that the second of the two did not contain pencils, and that 'I should not forget to tell Uncle F. that when he comes again.' Not until I had promised to do so did he calm down about this."

**5;4** Further examples from the diary: "G. committed two misdeeds while we were traveling. One of these (a clumsy handling of a stick) happened 'by accident,' as he himself emphasized, and as was confirmed by others who were there. But now as the second misdeed was understood by the parents as something that also had happened 'by accident,' the truth-loving boy admitted: '*The thing with Hilde was not an accident*.'

"The concept of lie is still not fully clear to him; he still does not know its limits, but instead extends it too broadly. But just now he seems to be right in the middle of the task of working out the correct way to understand this. Previously, when I had had the occasion to make clear to him what a lie is, I admonished him repeatedly: 'One must speak about everything as it really is.' He concludes from this: 'Whatever is said that does not—or does not any longer—match reality is a lie.' In the evening of the day before yesterday, he called out of the dark room: '*Mother please come, I want to tell you something. When we were at Aunt T.'s in Berlin, I said that I wanted to become a doctor. But now I don't want to be a doctor, so that was a lie.*' I calmed him and explained that he had not lied, because at the time he really did want to be a doctor, and now he had changed his mind. I told him that I would write to his aunt and tell her that he no longer wanted to become a doctor."

**5;4** His understanding of truth is such that he cannot accept even untruths told in jest. Yesterday, as we parents returned home from a walk with the children, I suggested to Hilde: "Go up and say that you children returned home alone from the walk. Else (the nanny) will be amazed." Hilde laughed and agreed to this: but Günter said: "*No, I won't say that, that is a lie.*"

He even protects himself against statements that might in the future prove false. He had hit his little sister on the head. I forbade him to do that, explaining to him the possible damage he could cause, and when I was finished I asked him: "So you won't do that any more, right?" Answer: "*I don't know.*" He said this not at all obstinately or defiantly, but on the contrary most contritely. He had tears in his eyes, but he knew his own impulsiveness too well to trust himself to make a firm promise for the future that he might not be able to keep.

**6;0** To sum up, we can say of Günter at the end of his 6th year: "He now understands the concept of a lie. His love of truth is unchanged, but it no longer expresses itself through an exaggerated anxiousness. Nevertheless, he still quite regularly adds such expressions as '*perhaps*, '*I think*,' or '*I can't say for sure*' to his statements, and is also quite strictly critical of his younger sister when she, in a fashion appropriate for her age, confuses what is with what appears to be the case."

The mother of the girl Y, who in her 5th year had repeatedly lied (see p. 114), claims that she is now a truth fanatic. The present writer herself witnessed the following scene: Y came home from a visit. Her mother asked her if she had been a good girl, to which she immediately answered, "*But I did this again,*" and raised her hand to her nose. Then she made a very unhappy expression and broke into tears, assuring her mother that she just did not know why she kept doing that. In the same way, she immediately admits it when she has bickered with a friend or broken something.

# III

## PRACTICAL APPLICATIONS[33]

# 11

## EDUCATING YOUNG CHILDREN TO REPORT ON THEIR EXPERIENCES

The study of the development of testimony and recollection in early childhood has brought forth the same results as those obtained with older children and with adults: The ability to testify about things that have been experienced is limited both by genuine deficiencies and by deliberate falsifications. Once these limitations became apparent, the question arose about whether or not they could be redressed or at least reduced. The age-old excuse for incomplete or incorrect testimonials—in other words, that they result from a "bad memory" to which one must simply resign one's self—has shown itself to be untenable. "Bad memory" is merely a catch-all notion for a great many psychological phenomena that are quite different from one another and that are, in greatly varying degrees, susceptible to influence. Some of these phenomena cannot even properly be regarded as functions of memory. They are instead functions of observational skills and of will, and are thus only some of the factors contributing to recollection. But with respect to precisely these factors children can be educated, and in this way their ability to recall material can be enhanced.

Up to this time, the pedagogical challenges in the area of recollection and testimony that arise from these considerations have been considered only with respect to their application within the schools.[34] The idea is similar to the notion, formulated more than a century ago, that perceptual skills could be trained, insofar as both notions assume the possibility of training a psychological function through the application of didactic methods. Just as voices in opposition to this notion were raised at that time, arguing that one does not have to learn to perceive and instead simply does this naturally, so might we expect some opposition to the notion that children can profitably be instructed in the domains of recollection and testimony. Yet already results from studies along these lines that have been carried out in schools show that pedagogy in testimony promises to become a valuable part of overall education. In truth, the full effects of this pedagogy will not be realized until such measures are implemented before the school years, in the children's play rooms at home and in the kindergartens. Here, we need concern ourselves only with the matter of this very early education in testimony and recollection.

Obviously, we are not dealing with a matter of systematic instruction or school-type mastery of a subject. In an altogether natural way, the opportunities for instructing young children must be exploited—for example, while taking walks, during play, while looking at pictures, while telling stories, while musing over various recollections. In these contexts, the testimonial errors, suggestive effects, and so forth that occur offer especially good material for analysis and evaluation.

The effort to improve testimonial deficiencies can begin either with the initial impression or with its reproduction.


## TRAINING CHILDREN TO OBSERVE

On average, children are good observers in many contexts. For them, after all, the world offers much more novelty and occasion for wonderment than it does for the indifferent adult. As a result, observations that children immediately and spontaneously express are often surprisingly accurate. But there are also constraints: the limited understanding that children bring to many of their impressions, their fleeting attentiveness, their rapid distractability, their inability to grasp properly the spatial, temporal, and logical connections between isolated experiences. As a result, their observations often lack both the accuracy that is necessary for correct subsequent recollection and the durability through which those observations can be filled out and detailed and become embedded into their lasting store of memoric images.

It is here where the work of the educator must begin. The adult can explain much to children that would otherwise escape their understanding, and this is why the adult should become involved with the child at the time of initial observation. The adult can invite the child to linger a bit longer over some object of observation and induce the child to seek out ever more characteristic features of what is being examined. The adult can have the child indicate what is similar and different about several objects being observed. The adult can induce the child to notice—or better yet, let the child discover on her own—how appearances change under different conditions, and how a particular object is part of some larger context. While viewing some object, the adult can allow his or her own errors of observation to be corrected.

A good way to discover deficiencies of observation is to have a 4- to 6-year-old child draw something "from memory," because children at this age are hardly able to simply copy something. Even the simplest figure drawn by a child reveals the child's knowledge of the object, and if the camel's hump looks like a chimney, it at least reveals that the child noticed the hump. On the other hand, the adult might be most surprised to see a four-legged bird, which would reveal how limited the child's observation has been.

The behavior of the adult in the face of the spontaneous curiosity and questioning of the child is very important. When the child excitedly brings a little flower or stone to show what he or she has found, and to learn the word and concept for it, this is something that can have a lasting positive influence on the pleasure the child takes in observing his or her world. But repeated dismissal of the child can snuff out this inquisitiveness at a very early age.

In and of itself, educating children to observe serves a worthy purpose that has been recognized for a long time. In kindergartens, for example, much is invested in nurturing just this function. No less important, however, is its intermediate function with respect to the education of children's ability to give testimony. A child can give good testimony only about something that has been carefully observed to begin with. If our own children did well in studies in which they were asked to report on what they had seen in pictures, this is partly because they learned at an early age not to just skim pictures but instead to attend to them thoroughly. In like fashion, one need only sit down with children and a picture book to see what happens in studies of testimony after the pictures have been looked at. At first, the child must relate spontaneously everything he sees, and then he must in turn ask the questions that, to the best of his own knowledge, are the ones needing answers. If one does not allow the child to begin on his own, and instead completely directs the child from the very beginning, the latter's interest in the exercise, which is a precondition for sustained attention, will soon disappear. Only when the child cannot find anything more on his own should one seek to prompt the child's spontaneity once again through questions about further details of the picture, about the activities of the persons or animals in the picture, about colors, and so forth. Obviously, one should do this only so long as the child truly remains attentive. In this context, the adult must be able to sense the right moment to introduce a change or to interrupt the exercise.

As essential as pictures are to this effort toward early childhood education in observation, even more so are objects that are at hand everywhere, both indoors and outdoors. However, the adult him- or herself must have a talent for and interest in observation to provide the most influential educational influence of all: example. A simple coffee bean that the mother lays before the child is seen quite differently, because it is examined, described, and discussed in isolation. Cautiously, a child brings a beetle: What can the child learn by examining the bug when the adult looks on and guides, and in the process says what she or he knows about the critter. While climbing a high mountain, the child notices, perhaps spontaneously, that at different places the trees look different, that sometimes the branches extend in only one direction, and so forth. The adult provides the context by showing how in this matter the wind and weather can be influential, and in this way guides the child to pay attention to other confirmatory instances of these effects.

**3;8** The contagious effect of example is something we experienced one summer with our youngest daughter. Her older siblings were accustomed to standing on the balcony and taking note of every change in the wind, the light, and the colors in the countryside. For her part, Eva would get excited about pointing out the areas of sunshine in the distance, or, with the pride of a discoverer, the pockets of fog in the mountains.

## TRAINING CHILDREN TO REPORT ACCURATELY ON PAST EVENTS

It is even more true of children than of adults that most of what is experienced is lost, at least in the sense that it cannot be reproduced. But even that which can be reproduced is not necessarily available to one without taking other factors into consideration. Often, a considerable effort of will is necessary to raise a stored recollection above the threshold. As discussed in chapter 6, this activity of bringing to mind an idea corresponding to some past experience is something that the child is able to do, at least to a limited degree, from the 4th year of life on. In this connection, the child's caretaker often has to overcome a certain tendency of the child to take the easy way out in response to the challenge "think about it" by simply saying "I don't know." At first, one teaches the child to concentrate: One hinders the child from allowing him- or herself to submit to other distractions (e.g., one removes the child's toy for the moment, and guides the child in a logical way toward finding her own way back to the latent memory).

As a test of this, we made use of part of a set of memories that for Günter were interrelated. We did this several days after an expedition in the mountains, and we note that, in this instance, some small prompts were necessary to fill in some gaps.

6;2    G. reported correctly on most things, but made no mention at all of an important place (the big lake). Mother: "You forgot one major point: Where were we before we came to Prince Heinrich's cabin?" G.: "*Maybe I didn't see that.*" M.: "Oh yes." G.: "*Did I discover it?*" (which means, was I the first of the group to notice it?) M.: "No, but you were one of the first." G.: "*No, I don't know.*" M.: "You threw stones there." G.: "*Oh yes, the big lake. We were on our way up.*" M.: "Don't you know anything else about the big lake?" G.: "*We splashed around there and threw stones, to see who could throw the farthest. Father and Mr. St. threw stones, too.*" M.: "Doesn't anything else come to mind about the big lake?" G.: "*Do you know anything else?*" M.: "So much amazed us when we were there." G.: "*The lake took on all sorts of colors as we went up, sometimes bright blue and sometimes green. And then we went to a place where there were big stones, and we sat on them and looked down at the lake. Then you (and some others in the party) finally arrived, you were the last ones, Father and I were the first; and then we went to Prince Heinrich's cabin.*"

Sometimes it is possible to prompt a reconstruction motorically. Suppose that a child can no longer remember where she has left some or other object. She might wish to retrace her steps so that, in the process, it will occur to her where she was last in possession of the object, and thus where the object might have been put down. In this connection one can refer to the incident discussed earlier (p. 67) involving our daughter Eva's search for the key. Here is another example of how motoric movement can sometimes be the basis for bringing something to mind:

6;2    Günter had tried to determine how long he could stand on one leg, and after a few minutes wanted to repeat the experiment with the other leg. But he raised the same leg as he had the first time, and we could not convince him of this. At this point, we challenged him to go to the place where he had carried out the first experiment, to stand facing the same direction as he had been facing, and then think about it. Immediately, he was able to recall his original position, and recognized his subsequent error.

In these instances of motoric "retracing of steps," we were dealing with very recent happenings. In the vast majority of such cases, however, the searching and finding must be carried out in imagination. In such instances, the caretaker who would prompt such recollections runs the danger of posing leading questions. In any case, such questions are usually avoided when one makes the effort not to force ideas onto the child but instead just to help the child find his own way. We recommend that the caretaker, in instances involving pedagogical objectives, engage the child in exercises for recalling only material with which the caretaker him- or herself is familiar, so that the latter can exercise some control over that which the child achieves. Because only then can the caretaker see through false testimonials or fantastic reconstructions and nip them in the bud. If inquiries are made about things one does not know about, then one can easily end up with the opposite of what was intended: a reinforcement not of the ability to bring things correctly to mind but instead of the tendency to confabulate or just to forget about things.

At this point we encounter a factor whose influence in the entire area of testimony, the accurate as well as false,[35] can have fateful consequences. The major finding throughout the psychology of testimony is that material related spontaneously is more correct than material produced in response to questioning, and that the way in which questions are phrased influences the answers that are given. The practical implications for pedagogy are easy to see. It is not necessary to avoid all questioning, but one must question carefully, and only after the child has finished saying whatever he can recall spontaneously. One does not ask about things that in all likelihood are out of the range of the child's interest and observation (compare in this regard the examples given in the next chapter). Above all one should avoid leading questions—that is, those that incline the person being questioned toward one answer rather than another.[36] The caretaker must be able to be sufficiently objective that she or he does not "put into the child's mouth" what she or he regards as probable or preferable, for example through questions such as, "Isn't it true that Paul is the person whom you last saw with the ball?"

The suggestibility of children is widely variable. There are many for whom simple questions, which in terms of their form are not at all leading, nevertheless induce a confirmatory response. There are other children— among whom is our Eva—who maintain their convictions even in the face of quite strongly leading questions.

Naturally, it is important for the caregiver to know the extent to which the child in his or her care is susceptible to influence. Apart from the experiences of day-to-day living, it is possible to carry out little experiments that can be informative in this regard. For example, after looking at pictures or at the end of other activities, various questions can be asked, with purposively suggestive questions intermixed among them.

Beyond this, however, the same sorts of experiments can be carried out specifically for pedagogical purposes in the area of child testimony, and that is their more important goal.

The usual way of reproaching false testimony: "You're wrong, it was not this way, but that way," usually has only a superficial effect. The correction either fails altogether in the face of the child's conviction to the contrary, because the correction simply was not convincing, or else the child surrenders only with reference to the specific instance in question. Under these circumstances, the child does not gain any deeper insight into the inadequacy of his or her performance, and so in subsequent similar instances is no more circumspect than before.

What the merely authority-based claim of the caregiver cannot accomplish, however, is accomplished by presenting the child with incontrovertible evidence. This is why studies using pictures are so valuable, especially with young children. Only in this way can one achieve an unobjectionable confrontation between the source of the child's impression (i.e., the picture) and the testimony given about it (compare chapter 8). If a child is asked about the contents of a picture that has previously been seen and then subsequently shown the picture, there is no way for the child to fail to recognize her own mistakes. The caregiver can take advantage of the child's surprise to teach the child how easy it is to make mistakes, and to explain to him or her that when one is not completely sure of something, it is better to say "I don't know" than to pretend to be certain. The caregiver can draw the child's attention to the specific areas in which mistakes were made, so that the child will pay closer attention to such details in the future. Warnings can also be given, in a form suitable for a child, of course, about the effects of leading questions. One might say, "I asked if a lamp was in the picture. If you're no longer certain if you've seen a lamp or not, it is okay to simply say 'I don't know.' "

In this confrontation between what is seen and what is said about what is seen, things must be arranged as much as possible so that the child's spontaneity accomplishes the initial work. One should not be hasty to point out the child's mistakes, but should instead allow the child to find them on her own. Self-correction of the deviations of performance from the ideal makes a much deeper impression than does correction by another person. Beyond this, the feeling of shame that often arises when a child is confronted with evidence of her own failure can be compensated by the satisfaction of finding one's own mistakes.

Regarding picture experiments, the objection is often raised that they are too artificial to be relevant to real life. Our analysis shows, however, that from a pedagogical standpoint pictures are necessary. At this age, everything depends on the comparison between a child's testimony and the incontrovertible evidence provided by the picture itself. Investigative procedures that are closer in respects to everyday life (e.g., a walk, a game), do not offer a criterion of truth convincing enough for the small child. If one repeats the activity for the purpose of demonstrating a mistake in testimony, the child can still claim, in characteristically childish obstinacy, that things were different the first time.

Only investigations that make use of real objects (e.g., a flower, a coin, a book) or of constant object relations (specifically, spatial—e.g., the position of furniture in a room, the configuration of a landscape) can replace those that employ pictures. For example, one could have a child describe how the furniture in an adjoining room is situated and then send the child into the room to see if his description was correct. (Compare the example involving Hilde, p. 30.) Alternatively, one could entice a child who has been in the mountains for several weeks and has had a more or less constant opportunity to observe the skyline with its various markers to sketch an outline on paper. The point would not be the artistic adequacy of the drawing but rather the accuracy of the recollection—that is, whether or not the major visible summits and ravines, public buildings, and so forth, have been placed in their approximately correct positions. Following this, one should check the child's production against the actual scene.

# 12

## THE ORIGINS OF LYING
## AND ITS PREVENTION

Different perspectives on the moral aspects of early childhood are nowhere in greater conflict than with respect to the pedagogical problem presented by lying. On one hand, the belief prevails that the small child is by nature not merely amoral but indeed antimoral, and that therefore lying is among the earliest manifestations of an egoism that has yet to be brought under control. On the other hand, there is the conviction that the naiveté of the child entails an innocence and lack of guilt, and that therefore the caretakers alone must bear the responsibility for the child's lies: "*Tout est bien sortant des mains de l'auteur des choses; tout dégénère entre les mains de l'homme*" ("Everything is good when it leaves the hands of the creator, but degenerates in the hands of man") (Rousseau).

We are dealing, then, with the opposition that in contemporary terminology we refer to with the words *nativism* and *empiricism*. In the former view, lying is regarded as something inborn, and in the latter view it is regarded as something entirely conditioned by the child's milieu. But as we have tried to show in chapter 10, a psychogenetic perspective on lying shows that neither of these extreme positions is correct. Instead, just like every other psychological function, lying must be seen as a consequence of the convergence of inner and outer causal factors.[37] Our task at this point, especially with regard to pedagogical practices with small children, is to determine the relative influence of these two factors, and to thereby ascertain the most apt means to prevent lying.

In the foregoing analysis we have tried to clarify the psychological factors involved when a child lies. In doing so, we have found that lying is such a complex phenomenon, and so variable in its nature from one instance to another, that it would be erroneous to regard lying per se as a natural tendency. On the other hand, there are certain basic factors that contribute to lying and to truthfulness and that may be regarded as tendencies immanent in the child in variable degree.

First, and most important of these, is the survival instinct, which causes the child to defend him- or herself against any threatening unpleasantness or danger.

Second, there is the immanent tendency to allow the imagination to run freely, and in a playful manner independent of reality. This is the tendency toward fantasy.

Third, there is the natural propensity to imitate. At an early age this propensity is manifested in the child's indiscriminate imitation not only of things that are worthy of imitation but also of things that are not.

Fourth, we may mention the tendency to evaluate, which in this context means the tendency to approve and disapprove of one's own motives and actions as well as those of others. But this ability is formal in nature. The particular content of what is regarded as good or bad depends on external factors to be discussed later on.

Fifth, the child is possessed of a natural tendency to transform its evaluative appraisals into the motives of its own will.

Sixth, there is a certain dynamic feature of the will: The more dependent and the weaker the child's will is, the more easily the child surrenders to the pressure of suggestive influences, whatever form the latter might take. On the other hand, the more independent and the stronger the child's will, the more he or she is able to maintain its position even in the face of suggestive influences.

But all of these inborn tendencies are merely formal and dynamic possibilities for activity, and hence always merely contributing factors. To be sure, each can contribute to a greater or lesser tendency toward truth-telling or lying in proportion to its degree of presence within the person. In all cases, however, the effects of such tendencies are augmented by other contributing factors in determining a specific component of psychological life and a particular orientation toward truth-telling.

This determination also involves outer factors: The milieu, which can exert training—or mistraining—effects of which the child is quite unconscious, child-rearing practices in general, and, lastly, efforts aimed directly at preventing and dealing with lying.

There is no stronger argument for the great influence of outer circumstances on the appearance or absence of lying than the fact that children of the educated classes lie much less, on average, than those of lower socioeconomic levels. For even on the hypothesis that children of the proletariat inherit dispositions that leave them less resistant to influences that precipitate lying—a question we will not pursue here—these same children are just the ones exposed in greatest number to those [untoward environmental] influences. To an extraordinary degree, the child of lower socioeconomic status is left to rely on him- or herself, and as a result is exposed to the suggestive influences of peers who are likewise drifting or already ruined. The child of lower socioeconomic status is thus exposed to all sorts of enticements, is lured to the fringes of society, and then faces hard, often brutal and unjustified penalties administered without sufficient appreciation for these background factors. Is not hitting, used not as punishment but instead simply as the expression of unmitigated anger, unfortunately still today the preferred child-rearing method of the proletariat? It is no wonder that under such circumstances the child resorts to lying in self-defense. Moreover, how many children in the big cities are nowadays actually forced by their parents into lying? Five-year-old children are made to go door to door and tell a fabricated story of misery in hopes of obtaining sympathetic handouts.

Perhaps these same children who resort to lying would, were they to be raised in an educated, orderly, and more nurturant environment, remain nonliars. The examples given in chapter 10 show that there can be environments in which lying does not occur. But even in educated circles, circumstances are not always such that the younger generation is exposed to exemplary influences. Unfortunately, there are indeed families in which the entire lifestyle is based on lying and deception. For example, even little children can sense the essential untruthfulness that exists in impoverished families who live above their means. The children themselves are at times called on to conceal as much as possible the deficiencies of their sustinence and clothing.

Even the much more harmless "white lies" that children must listen to, or into which they are sometimes even recruited (e.g., being told to say that "Mother is not at home" when mother does not wish to be visited) perhaps draw the child's attention for the first time to the fact that there is such a thing as an intentional deviation from the truth. In any case, these experiences deprive children of their unquestioning trust in what adults say.

It is surprising to see how highly educated persons engage in activities that they regard as harmless to their children. To save 10 cents on the streetcar, a mother will risk damaging what is most precious in the child. She requires the child to lie about his age, and in the process she herself sows the seeds of untruthfulness. Then later, when the same child lies to his mother at home, he will receive a lecture about lying and will be punished: "Children's lies are the work of the child-raiser" (Rousseau).

Another group of "white lies" perpetuated by parents, caretakers, and relatives can exert its effect among still younger children and, as harmless as they might seem, can have such undesirable consequences. We are referring to those pretenses, sometimes carried out with 1-year-old children, through which the latter are supposed to be momentarily diverted, consoled, confused, frightened, or calmed down—for example, "If you're bad, the boogie man will get you!" or "If you're good, I'll give you some chocolate!" (without then keeping the promise) or, "Look, there is a cat!" which is not really there (to get the crying child to think about something else). Parents should avoid such pretenses altogether, and should further see to it that others charged with caring for the child are so instructed. Yet most parents are not even aware of this basic pedagogical principle.

Scupin's diary records are instructive in this connection. From them we learn that the mother and household help drew up lists of threats and diversions to be used with the child. Thus, as a result of a foolish and untrue story told by the nanny, the boy manifested at ages 1;8 and again at 1;11 great fear of a "Boogie man" who was supposedly living behind the oven [1907, pp. 80 & 90]. Then in the place of this "Boogie man" when the boy was in his 3rd year, he started talking about "spiders" [1907, pp. 116 & 207], which he believed were in the rooms. For a time the fear of spiders even became a dominant issue for him. In this light, it is hard to understand why for a long time the mother herself used pretenses involving spiders. She writes [1907, p. 203]:

**2;11** "If mother wants to wash the boy's head while bathing him, for 6 months she has relied on a trick that never fails to get Bubi to look up, so that the soapy water does not run into his eyes. She says to him: 'Look up at the ceiling, there is a spider up there!' Every time, he looks up intently, and sometimes even claims to see the spider."

It is possible in this case that, for a while, the boy's anxious fantasy deceived him, but the following case undoubtedly sowed mistrust. The boy was photographed "with a funny expression on his face as he looked with breathless attention in reaction to having been told that there was a chicken under the photographer's black cloth that would come out and crow. Poses for the additional photographs proved to be more difficult to achieve, as Bubi became frustrated when the chicken would not come out [1907, p. 201]. One can compare this observation with an analogous case showing how an event involving photography was handled in the case of our daughter Eva [see p. 58].

Perhaps many would say that it is pedantic to criticize such small deceptions when they are used to help manage children. But quite apart from the untoward effect on the child's psychological equilibrium that the pretense of frightening things can have, it can also cause mistrust of one's surroundings to creep into the consciousness of children who are treated this way. When a child finally grasps more or less clearly that he is often deceived (spiders on the ceiling when the hair is being washed, a chicken under the black cloth used by the photographer), the tendency toward imitation can soon lead to little deviations from truth on the child's part. At the age of 1 yr. and 11 months, the Scupin boy already shows mistrust of his mother [Scupin & Scupin, 1907, p. 97]. "In response to his continuous request for cake, mother told him that there was no more in the drawer. With that he made gestures of displeasure ... he cried, 'No, open, see!'" And it has already been noted in chapter 10 that from time to time the boy resorts to small lies despite the sincere efforts of his parents.

**2;6**   Concerning his son, Lindner [1898, p. 79] also relates an example of that early mistrust that can arise from playing tricks on children that they do not understand: "He rarely believes what others around him say, but instead and whenever possible he will investigate the matter himself." Lindner believes that the boy's sister has often told him things in jest that were not true, and that he has now generalized his mistrust to his parents without the latter even having given him reason to do so. In another incident 2 months after the one just noted, the boy would not calm down "until his mother allowed him to inspect for himself a basket in which he had supposed there were pretzels."

The actions of others around the child that we have mentioned up to now suggest that lying in children could arise through imitation. But this is not the only cause, or even the most important one. Because even in the most rigorous families in which every untruth whatsoever is painstakingly avoided, especially in the presence of children, the children can still become deceitful. This can happen just because of that very rigor, which often dominates other aspects of life as well and in turn leads to untoward pedagogical practices. Too many proscriptions and false strictness breed deceit. Even the child who is otherwise predisposed to behave well must resort to lying when that child is repeatedly forbidden to do things and is threatened with harsh penalties for every little infraction.

Out of convenience, and often out of exaggerated anxiousness, child-rearing is for many parents or caretakers an endless list of proscriptions. The child is denied the most innocent of wishes, either because mother has no time just now, or because the new game the child wants to play requires preparation, or because the adult does not want the child to get dirty or to clutter up the room, or because the child might hurt him- or herself or catch a cold, or because of this or that other reason. The more numerous and more senseless these proscriptions are, the more frequent become the violations, and the more frequent the occasions for punishment. At this point we encounter a second convenience to which many parents resort: They use their power to discipline blindly. They make no effort to understand the partial justification provided by the circumstances that led to the child's transgression. They do not try to be the prudent judge who seeks to make the punishment fit the crime, and in whose view admissions of offenses mandate milder punishments. In many cases, the punishments adults mete out are a projection of their own anger. As a result, the punishments are not properly graded, and they are administered without sufficient consideration for their consequences. Punishment should make the child "frightened"—yes, but of what? Sometimes, as intended, they frighten the child from repeating the act, but often they only frighten the child from admitting the repetition. The child's entirely natural survival tendencies incline him or her to resort to the only means available in the face of further punishment: lying. There are also adults who in their child-rearing practices do not even act in a manner consistent with juridical practice, according to which milder punishments are meted out to delinquents who admit to their offenses. Indeed, there are even those adults who promise such milder punishments to gain a confession, and then themselves become liars by not keeping their word. Again we see the truth of Rousseau's claim: "The lies of the child are the work of the child-rearer."[38]

In those (unfortunately too frequent) legal proceedings in which parents or child-rearers are accused of child abuse, the adults almost always claim that the children are liars and incorrigible. This is often the case. But if one follows up these cases, one sometimes discovers that children who have been removed from the unhappy influences on them and placed into nurturant environments become open and truth-loving persons. In these cases, the deceitfulness of the children was simply a reaction to the brutality of the adults who had been raising them.

The opposite of extreme strictness is an exaggerated fussiness over the child. This, too, can lead to lying. An overly anxious mother who repeatedly asks the child if she needs something, or whether or not she has this or that pain and, when told yes, immediately does everything possible to make the child comfortable, or clears away what is unpleasant for the child provokes the child to claim just those sufferings asked about. In the long run, this leads to spontaneous claims on the child's part to be suffering in similar ways when she again wants to achieve something desired or avoid something unpleasant. Now and then, a confirmatory answer to fussy questioning might have a legitimate basis, but in other cases such an answer can simply occur as a consequence of suggestion. If a child's caretaker persists with such pampering questions, the child would have to be exceptionally strong willed and morally firm to maintain resistance for any extended period of time. On page 114, we discussed an example from the work of Marcinowski which illustrates the point we are making. It had to do with a child who regularly complained of "stomachaches" when a rice dish was served at mealtime. The manner in which Marcinowski describes such lies corresponds to the perspective we have sketched previously.[39]

But asking children questions must also be discussed independently of this pampering tendency. "One who asks many questions gets many answers," and the truth status of these answers is more problematic the more intrusive and relentless the questioning is. The literature pertaining to the psychology of testimony has already taught us this. But although that literature emphasizes that intrusive questioning leads to intentional falsifications, it must also be emphasized that such questioning is also a source of unconscious untruths. This holds for questioning of all kinds. There are, first of all, the apparently harmless questions of curiosity. Their intent is to obtain from the child news about her experiences that quite possibly have not been consciously "experienced" at all, or have long since been forgotten. Finally, the child submits to the pressure of the questioning only to please the questioner or to escape him or her, especially when the questioner rejects the answer "I don't know" and demands of the child specific answers. In this way, and without knowing it, many unreflective parents sow the seeds of fibbing and boasting when, for example, they greet the child returning home from a walk or from a visit somewhere with an unending sequence of questions about trivialities.[40]

This sort of inquisition merits even more attention when it is aimed at pinpointing guilt for something, be it that of a child or of another person. Even as an elderly man, Gottfried Keller remembers with bitterness an event from his childhood in which a woman he did not know pushed him into a web of lies as fateful as it was foolhardy. One can read his perceptive account of this in *Green Heinrich*, an account that should make clear to all parents and child-rearers the sorts of practices that are to be strictly avoided when questioning children [reprinted in Bäumer & Droescher, 1908, p. 109].

Our considerations so far relate to inappropriate pedagogical practices of a general nature (exaggerated strictness, pampering, inquisition) that lead to the development of lying. We now have to consider the principles of more positive ways of behaving, bearing specifically on the ways in which lying is handled.

First of all, in each instance in which a child makes a false statement one must be clear about whether the child is aware that the statement is false, whether the child has intended the statement seriously, and whether the statement is, from the child's perspective, self-serving. That is, one must be sure that the falsehood is a genuine lie. The adult is far too quickly inclined to project his or her own experiences onto the child; and because it is regularly the case that when an adult says something untrue she or he is lying, the adult also regularly concludes, in analogous fashion, that when the child says something untrue, the child likewise is lying. This reveals a regrettable deficit of psychological intuition, because as countless examples from chapter 10 show, one finds only traces of genuine lies in the many different apparent lies told by children in their first year of life. In most cases—and for many children in all cases—these pseudo-lies have their source in much more elementary psychological functions. We would not go so far as Jean Paul[41] to claim that "up to the age of 5 our children say nothing true and nothing false; they just speak," but we would say that under favorable conditions we would regard this statement as an accurate description of what is normal up to the age of 3 years.

That in specific instances the small child might receive an unwarranted punishment is not the only consequence of false interpretation and pedagogical overzealousness on the part of parents. What is perhaps worse is that the concept of a lie is forced onto the child at much too early an age. At a time during which naiveté and openness are entirely natural to the child, the little person should not be confronted at all with the fact that something like a contradiction between what is meant and what is said actually exists. There is no need for the word "lie" to be part of the vocabulary of a 2- to 3-year-old child. Even if at this age the child occasionally deviates considerably from the truth, a harsh "You're lying!" is certainly less helpful than a serious and age-appropriate discussion of the matter, perhaps in the way shown by the example on page 109. Questions that lead the child to discover on her own the difference between what has been seen and what has been said—for example, "Did you see the cook do so and so?" (refer to p. 111), and reminders to the child that one should always speak the truth, serve well. One should take care not to make too much of the isolated lie—to make a federal case of it—and this is a principle that should hold throughout pedagogy in early childhood. One should not constantly draw attention to small transgressions or bad habits and in this way only embed them more deeply in the child's psyche. Often, an intentional disregard of a transgression results in the latter just disappearing on its own.

In any given case, of course, the caretaker must behave in accordance with his or her feel for the particulars of that individual case. We can discuss only the psychological preconditions for this.

Naturally, the approach we are suggesting can only be successful when all who are involved work together. Hence parents must also indicate to any other adults who may come into regular contact with the child (relatives, babysitters, household help, and so forth) that accusations of lying are serious and require great circumspection.

Once a child reaches the age of 3 or 4 years, one can gradually appeal to her moral sensibilities and explain why lies are reprehensible and damaging. This can be done whether the goal is therapeutic or preventive. Regarding the latter, we have made good use in our nursery of stories that convey some moral. Some of these are well-known—for example, "The Little Shepherd Boy Who Cried 'Wolf!'" and "Fritz, Fritz, Look Out for the Bridge!" and some others we made up ourselves. The children understood them, and even made references to the stories on their own, in subsequent appropriate situations.

Because the literature already contains many older and more recent writings dealing specifically with moral pedagogy in the domain of children's lies, the previous remarks will suffice for this psychological work.

To summarize all that has been said to this point, the best defense against lying is, to borrow a notion from hygiene, a preventative one—in other words, one that does not simply wait until the sickness has broken out but instead stops it from ever getting started. But just as hygiene can develop into a kind of hygienic compulsiveness that, as a result of a constant fear of bacteria, would impose a thousand restrictions, impediments, and cautionary practices on a person, in this case, too, one must avoid excessiveness. Rousseau, for example, goes far too far when he teaches, in his *Émile*, that one should not demand the truth from a child and in the process induce the child to conceal the truth, or that one should not demand a promise so that it will not be broken, or that in the case of some or other incident one should never ask, "Did you do that?" and so forth. He states, "The more the child's well-being is made independent, be it of the will of others or of their judgment, the less will be the child's interest in lying." This artificial isolation, discussed in talk of "natural" childrearing, is essentially a kind of pampering that will exact its cost as soon as the unnatural conditions maintaining isolation no longer hold.[42] One can well understand Rousseau's pleas as a reaction to prevailing, overly strict child-rearing practices. But to the extent that he is struggling against excessive discipline, he also undermines, to a considerable extent, self-discipline; and it is precisely those child-rearing practices that foster self-discipline that offer the best possibility of recruiting the child him- or herself to the collective struggle against lying. Even in the most sheltered environment, real life does not insulate the child from the lies of others, or from his or her own attempts to lie. A child whose parents teach him about the importance of maintaining self-control in general, a child who has learned to curb his own anger, or to forego a pleasure out of consideration for others, or to tolerate an unfairness—yes, one who can take satisfaction in having achieved self—control—will also overcome his own inclinations to lie.

# 13

## THE CAPABILITY OF SMALL CHILDREN AS WITNESSES IN LEGAL PROCEEDINGS

The problem of testimony by children in legal proceedings is a very complicated one and confronts judges, pedagogues, and parents with many difficult tasks. These cases, it is clear, most often arise with children older than those with whom we have been concerned in this work. Nevertheless, we cannot overlook this topic entirely, because we know that, from time to time, we must deal with cases in which children of quite a young age must testify in a legal hearing.[43]

The considerations that speak against subjecting young children to legal hearings are of a two-fold nature: ethical and psychological.

A child that has herself been the victim of or witness to a crime has, in the process, suffered a disturbance to her psychological equilibrium, and those around the child should do everything possible to help the child overcome the experience. In other cases, we are talking about events that happened to the child beyond her own understanding (such as inappropriate fondling), and this fortuitous innocence is something that must be respected rather than disturbed. This consideration has not been sufficiently honored in hearing procedures as they have been practiced up to now. The embarrassing formalities of the repeated hearings by the police, the investigative judge, the court, the inevitably distasteful discussion of the matter, the necessity of giving an account of things that happened weeks or months previously, all of this contributes to the development of an ideational complex that remains and festers in the child's mind when it would have been more desirable for this material to recede out of awareness as quickly as possible. It is quite understandable that parents and caretakers sometimes decide against bringing charges following an offense committed against a child to avoid exposing children to the considerable effects of the legal hearing process. However, this gives rise to an ethical dilemma: To the extent that adults intend to protect as much as possible the children in their care, they impede the punishment of the perpetrator, who is in turn at liberty to seek new victims.

The psychological implications of the experimental results currently available are clear. They show that children are able to accurately observe and sometimes also able to correctly report on things, especially things that interest them. This is particularly true when the recollection is still fresh, and when the child is allowed to give his report freely and spontaneously. But in legal settings, the questioning of witnesses usually does not fall within the sphere of a child's interests, does not allow the child to report spontaneously, and also does not pertain to recollections that are fresh.

On the other hand, we have tried to discover those features of falsification that necessarily belong to the mechanisms of early childhood testimony. The influences of these mechanisms are even more pronounced in the setting of a legal hearing, as well as through the fact that judges do not have an extensive understanding of child psychology. As a consequence, the child is often not treated in an age-appropriate way. What is least problematic from the standpoint of evaluating the testimony is the possibility that that testimony contains genuine lies. This is because genuine lies are much easier to detect than unintended falsehoods. The forensic significance of our findings in this regard can be summarized as follows: Because the small child has little awareness of the seriousness of the past event, his tendencies to confuse fantasy and reality may be dangerously exacerbated by the pressure being imposed on him to say something certain. Under pointed and forceful questioning, the child will often simply let habitual associations take their course mechanically, or arbitrarily throw together memoric images from experiences of various previous times, as if those experiences all stemmed from the same single point in time specified for the child by the person doing the questioning. Under the force of questioning, there are many yes's and no's that have the appearance of confirming this or that, but that in reality might only be expressing wishes or fears or absent-mindedness or indifference, or serving a defensive purpose. The more suggestive the forceful questioning—that is, the more it is directed toward producing a specific answer—and the more it constrains the choice of alternative possibilities, the more untoward this effect will be. Judicial interrogation of a child typically will have been preceded by a domestic interrogation, the suggestive influence of which cannot be determined. That is, if something happens to a child, it would be most unusual if the affair were not first investigated at home, and "clarified" through pointed (and perhaps leading) questioning. Also, hearsay concerning what others supposedly experienced in the same incident easily becomes something that the child believes she has experienced herself. The effect of all of these influences can be still greater the longer the interval of time between the occurrence of the event and the hearing.

Given the foregoing considerations, it has been suggested that up to a certain age children should simply not be permitted to testify in legal matters. But this seems ill-advised to us, at least in cases that would involve severe penalties. For one thing, knowledge of such a restriction would directly encourage crimes against children. For another thing, a child is sometimes the primary (or perhaps even the only) witness,[44] and if we proceed on the principle that in a legal matter every lead is to be followed up, we must not forget that this holds also for leads that may be provided by the psychological traces that an event leaves behind in the mind of a child. In petty cases, obviously, children should not testify, because the possible usefulness of the testimony—which in any case would be more problematic—is incommensurate with the psychological disadvantages to which the child would be exposed by the hearing.

However, in cases in which a hearing must be held, it should be conducted in such a way that, on the one hand, the relevant recollection is carefully elicited without its being blurred or "smeared" in the process, and that, on the other hand, the disturbance to the child's psychological equilibrium caused by the hearing itself should be minimized. Regulations as well as the personal behavior of the judge toward the child have roles to play. Regarding the former, it would be desirable for regulations stipulating that child witnesses (including those much older than those on whom we have focused in this work) should be questioned in a causal and non–anxiety-provoking atmosphere as soon as possible after the experience in question and in a hearing held separately from the main proceeding. The questioning should be done by an individual whose personality is especially well-suited to the task.

The fact that the differential legal treatment of young persons is increasing in our times might well contribute to the realization of the foregoing recommendations. If up to now these legal reforms based on child psychology have primarily concerned those cases in which young persons have been perpetrators of offenses, it would seem logical that consideration of young persons as witnesses in legal proceedings would have to follow. This new trend gives hope for the notion of a generation of judges under whose leadership legal hearings involving children will be conducted in more age-appropriate ways: through eliminating all superfluous formalities, through an individualized approach appropriate for a child, through encouraging spontaneous reporting, through consciously avoiding suggestive influences and leading questions, and through strictly psychological means of checking what the child says.

This is not the place to discuss in detail the techniques that should be employed in legal hearings involving children. It must suffice to have pointed to some general considerations.

# APPENDIXES

## Breakfast Picture: Scoring Summary

| Content of the picture | Hilde | | Günter | | Eva | |
|---|---|---|---|---|---|---|
| | P | S | P | S | P | S |
| woman | *(t)* | *(t)* | *(t)* | *(t)* | *(t)* | *(t)(f)f* |
| stands | *(t)* | *(t)* | *(t)* | *(t)* | *t* | *t* |
| to right of boy | *t* | | *t* | | | |
| holds bread | *t* | *(t)* | *(t)t* | *t* | *f* | *ft* |
| looks at the bread | | | *t* | | | |
| blue dress | *(t)\*(f)* | *(t)\** | *t\*f* | *t\*f* | | |
| red apron | *(t)\*(t)* | *(t)\*(t)* | *t\*t* | *t\*t* | *tf\** | *tf\** |
| without lace around edges | *t\*\** | *t\*\** | *u* | *t\*\** | | |
| with bib but without shoulder straps | *t* | *t* | *f* | *t* | | |
| brown hair | *(t)\** | *(t)\** | *t\** | *t\** | | |
| seen from the side | *t* | *t* | *t* | *t* | | |
| no knife in her hand | *t\*\** | *t\** | | *(f)t* | *t\*\** | *ft\*\** |
| knife | *t* | *t* | *(t)* | *(t)* | | |
| lying on table | *t* | *t* | *(t)* | *t* | *f* | *f* |
| bread | *t* | *(t)* | *(t)* | *(t)* | *t* | *t* |
| the usual shape | *t* | *t* | *t* | | | |
| light and dark brown | *t\** | *t\** | *t* | | | |
| sliced | *t* | *t* | *t* | *t* | | |
| sitting on the table | *t* | *t* | | *t* | *t* | *t* |
| table | *t* | *(t)* | *(t)* | *(t)* | *t* | *t* |
| light brown | *t\** | *t\** | *t* | *t\** | | |
| rectangular | *t* | *t* | *t* | *t* | | |
| no butter on the table | *t\*\** | *t\*\** | *t\*\** | *t\*\** | *t\*\** | *t\*\** |
| boy | *(t)* | *(t)* | *(t)* | *(t)* | *(t)* | *(t)* |
| sits | *(t)* | *(t)* | *(t)* | *(t)* | *t* | *t* |
| at the table | *(t)* | *(t)* | *(t)* | *(t)* | *t* | |
| on a stool | *t* | *t* | *(t)* | *(t)* | *t* | *t* |
| green jacket | *f\** | *(f)\** | *f\** | *f\** | *t* | *t* |
| dark red pants | *f\** | *(t)\** | *f\** | *t\** | *t* | *t* |
| not barefoot | *t\*\** | *t\*\** | *t\*\** | | *t\*\** | *t\*\** |
| blue stockings | *tf\** | *tf\** | *tf\** | *f* | *t* | *t* |
| black shoes | *tf\** | *f* | *tt\** | *t\** | *t* | *t* |
| oxford style | *t* | | *f* | *t* | | |
| holds feet on slats | *f* | *f* | *u* | *t* | | |
| he is eating | *(t)* | *(t)* | *(t)* | *(t)* | *t* | *t* |
| a piece of bread | *(t)* | *(t)* | *(t)* | *(t)* | *t* | *t* |
| light and dark | | | *t\** | | | |
| not whole | *t* | | | | | |
| no plate | *t* | | | | | |
| holds between thumb, index finger | *t* | *t* | *t* | *t* | *t* | *t* |

*Appendix A continues*

| Content of the picture | Hilde | | Günter | | Eva | |
|---|---|---|---|---|---|---|
| | P | S | P | S | P | S |
| dark blonde | (t)* | (t)* | t*/2; f*/2 | t* | | |
| seen from the side | t | t | t | t | | |
| stool | (t)(f) | t | (t) | (t) | t | t |
| with holes | (t) | | | | | |
| door | t | t | (t) | (t) | (t) | (t) |
| open | f | t | (t) | (t) | t | t |
| one panel | t | t | t | t | | |
| one cannot see anything outside | | | t** | t** | t** | f** |
| no window | t** | t | f** | (f) | t** | t** |
| behind the woman | | | (t) | | | |
| trunk | (t) | (f) t | (f) | (t) | t | t |
| by the wall | (t) | | | | | |
| to the right | t | t | t | t | | |
| wooden | (t) | | | | | |
| not entirely visible | t | (t) f | t | t | | |
| occluded by the woman | t | | f | f | | |
| flower pot | f | (t) | (t) | (t) | (t) | t |
| on the trunk | | (t) | (t) | (t) | t | t |
| geraniums with foliage | | t | (t) | (t) | | |
| red | | t* | t* | t* | | |
| green leaves | | t* | | | | |
| pot is red | | | t*/2 | t* | | |
| saucer | | | f | f | | |
| satchel | (t) | (t) | t | (t) | t | (t) |
| on the floor | (t) | | | (t) | t | t |
| next to the stool | (t) | (t) | t | | | |
| to the left | | | | t | | |
| red | (t)* | (t) | f* | f* | f* | |
| fitted top | | | | f | | |
| straps (of satchel) visible | f | (f) | | | | |
| mug | f | t | t | (t) | f | f |
| on the floor | | t | | (t) | | |
| under the stool | | f | t | (t) | | |
| green | | f* | f* | f* | | |
| speckled | | | t | (t) | | |
| one handle | | t | t | f | | |
| no top | | t** | f** | f** | | |

Letters in parentheses refer to correctness or incorrectness of statements made by children in their initial reports; letters outside of parentheses refer to correctness or incorrectness of statements made by children in response to questioning; $t$ = true; $f$ = false; $u$ = undetermined; * = statement about color; ** = answers to suggestive questions; P = primary report; S = secondary report.

Picture of Geese: Scoring Summary

| Content of picture | Hilde | Günter | Eva |
|---|---|---|---|
| maid | (t) | (t) | (t) |
| leads | (t) | (t) | |
| many geese | (t) | (t)(t) | (t) |
| on a walk | | | (t) |
| holds in her hand | | (t) | |
| a stick | t | (f) | (f) |
| top with branches | t | | |
| red skirt | f* | (t)* | f* |
| black apron | (f)*(t) | (f)*(t) | f* |
| white bonnet | f | t*t | t*t |
| wooden shoes | f | t | t |
| have open beaks | (t) | | |
| some in front, and some behind maid | t | | t |
| more behind | t | t | |
| yellow beaks | t* | t* | f* |
| yellow feet | f* | t* | f* |
| green meadow | (t)*(t) | t | |
| with flowers | t | t | |
| most as white spots | tt* | t | |
| some with smaller spots within | | f | |
| green trees | (t)t* | (t)*(t) | f |
| short trunks | t | t | |
| hardly visible | | t | |
| standing close together | t | f | |
| half-tree on the right | t | tf | |
| yellow fruit | tf* | (t)t* | t*t |

| Estimates | | | |
|---|---|---|---|
| 5½ trees | 5–6 | 6, 5, or 4 | |
| 3–4 fruits per tree | 5 | 10 | |
| 6 geese | 12 | 8 | |

Letters in parentheses refer to correctness or incorrectness of statements made by children in their initial reports. Letters outside of parentheses refer to correctness or incorrectness of statements made by children in response to questioning. $t$ = true; $f$ = false; * = statement about color.

# ENDNOTES

1. Compare in this regard Preyer [1905; section: Memory without words; Compayre [1900, p. 166 n.].

2. Preyer did not confirm a corresponding achievement of recognition in his child until about the age of 1¾ years [1905, p. 276]. On the other hand, Perez [1902, p. 78] reports of a 1-year-old child who, after a separation of a month, greeted his nanny happily.

3. A parallel to this is given in an observation made by Preyer [1905, p. 277] of his 2-year-old son; in this case, as well, the time taken to recognize playthings was several months (11½ weeks).

4. See W. Stern [1904, p. 125]. One should not be troubled by the fact that, with respect to the experiments discussed in this work, the three named stages were confirmed in their entirety at ages much later than those indicated in this case. After all, the stages do not signify the general developmental course of the psyche—of such a kind that the child in general thinks about everything in terms of substance at such and such an age, and then about everything in terms of action at such and such an age, and so on. Rather, the stages signify phases through which every kind of intellectual achievement itself passes. Achievements that according to their overall nature are proper to later ages will thus remain in the substance stages while others have long since reached the stage of action, and so on. Studies of schoolchildren have investigated behavior under the artificial and relatively difficult conditions of having to report on a picture no longer visible. This discussion deals with recollection capabilities under the easier conditions of everyday life. In the previously cited work [W. Stern, 1904, p. 128], it has already been indicated that with respect to another function, the learning of language, the succession of the three stages occurs at a still earlier age.

5. Compayre [1900, p. 171] paints a similar picture: "For the newborn child there is no depth extension. For the child who is some months old there is no perspective of the past."

6. Admittedly, such fine differentiations of recall remained rather isolated, even after this, so that even when the child was 3 years old we still found the following observation noteworthy:

> 3;0 "Upon returning from his walk, Father asked H. who had been present. H.: 'Robert.' Father: 'Who else?' H.: 'Certainly not the postman.' Asking about the postman is a regular occurrence in our house, which H. seems to have grasped already. Apart from the temporal differentiation, what is noteworthy is the opposition to suggestion and the correct negation of a recollection that was not requested at all.

7. Heller (1895) describes a very interesting analog to this in his "Studies in the Psychology of the Blind." When blind persons have progressively touched the contours of a large object—for example, a cabinet—they subsequently try to create a unified tactile illustration of the object by outlining it on such a reduced scale that it would then be possible to pick up the object with two hands.

8. Compare the example given on p. 14 and in monograph I (Children's Speech), p. 235, where Hilde's development of a concept of time and expressions is followed.

9. [W. Stern, 1904, p. 23]. In that case the research subjects were adults.

10. Translator's note: In the Sterns' original monograph, the spelling of the names of the Sterns' son changes from Günther to Günter. This change has been incorporated into the text of the translation.

11. The behavior of Hilde (who admittedly was 1 year older at the time) is comparable to these two cases [Preyer, 1905, p. 3].

12. Two completely unbelievable cases reported by Ament [n.d.] at least merit mention, because in a widely available popular pamphlet (*The Mind of the Child*) they are taken as paradigmatic cases for the earliest childhood recollections (or, as the case may be, recognitions). These cases have been discussed by others (e.g., Gaupp) and can be misused as illustrations. These are cases "which were recorded by an attentive child observer of absolute reliability." "Theodor, the hero of one case, chattered a great deal from the age of 5 months, primarily saying the syllables '*eyedyedyedyedye*.' Then his chattering stopped almost entirely. When after 6 months the child's grandmother came to visit, the mother complained to her that her boy had stopped chattering. The grandmother wanted to induce him to chatter again, and started uttering all kinds of syllables to him, including '*eyedye-dyedye*.' He did not react to any syllable except when she said '*eyedyedyedye*,' then he laughed with pleasure, yet without repeating the syllables." The interpretation is uncommonly arbitrary. That the child enjoyed hearing these well-known and much-loved sounds of affection is very likely, but that hearing them actually prompted the child to recall having heard them before seems more than improbable.

"In another case, a woman often sang to her 3- to 4-month old godchild the children's verse 'Three blind mice, three blind mice; see how they run, see how they run.' She left the child when she was 4 months old. Three quarters of a year later, when the child began to speak, she said '*hicky, dicky dock, mous uh clock*.' In the interim, the mother had never sung this verse to the child." No one who had actually observed the development of memory in children during the first year, and who would therefore know how beginning speakers express themselves, could regard as possible either a latency time of 9 months or a correct sound sequence of such length. Moreover, this verse is so widely known that the child could have heard it under any number of uncontrollable conditions, even when the mother was not involved.

13. That the sense of space has precedence is also clearly apparent in language development—for example, in the developmental sequence of space and time adverbs. See monograph *I* (*Children's Speech*), p. 23.

14. Major [1906, p. 215ff] makes a similar point.

15. In one case supposedly having to do with stored recollections from the prespeech period, the impressions were of an acoustic–linguistic nature rather than a visual nature. A girl observed by the medical practitioner Wolfert [1901] had spent the first year and a half of her life in Silesia, and as a result of complete neglect by her parents had remained speechless until the age of 2½. The girl was then taken from Silesia to Berlin, where she was closely cared for and developed quickly. "At the age of 5 years, the child suddenly began to use Silesian figures of speech, and intense research revealed that this could have had no origin other than her experiences in the early pre-speech period." (See Monograph 1, *Children's Speech*, p. 257.) Admittedly, this is an improbable case.

16. More on this topic will be reported in the monograph on the child's perception.

17. Indirect evidence that his perception of numbers is primarily visual is given by the fact that he notices the formal characteristics of the shapes of the numerals. For example, he noted of a 5 printed on a slant: "*It looks like it is resting*" and of a 6 printed straight up and down: "*It looks like it walks slowly.*" Even a 2 that he had inscribed himself prompted him to remark, laughingly: "*Oh how it runs.*"

18. Apart from purposive recall, there is also another activity of will aimed at the contents of memory, and that is the process of making "mental notes" of things. An early example of this is found on p. 17. The entire problem of learning is relevant, but it does not fit into the framework of this monograph.

19. There is a comprehensive literature concerning conscious and unconscious falsifications of testimony among schoolaged children, which we will not go into. The interested reader should consult the bibliographical citations at the end of the book.

20. It is an enlargement of the picture that is shown with the work by W. Stern [1902].

21. Purely experimental studies of statements about pictures bearing not only on one-time presentations but also continuous exposures will be discussed in chapter 8.

22. Lipmann and Wendriner [1906] set up testimony experiments in Kindergarten. Research subjects were six boys and six girls ages 4 to 6 years. Each child was asked nine questions about a picture that the child had just seen. The questions were divided into three groups according to the degree to which they were regarded as leading. Following a carefully specified sequence, it was possible to determine, for each of the pictured objects asked about, the effect of a more or less leading formulation of the question. This effect was quite clear. Questions that were only slightly leading, such as: "Is there a cabinet in the room?" (correct answer: no) were answered falsely 6% of the time. Mildly leading, or "expectant" questions (e.g., "Isn't there a cabinet in the room?") were answered falsely 25% of the time. Falsely assumptive and therefore highly leading questions (e.g., "Is the door of the cabinet open or closed?") were answered falsely 56% of the time. Girls performed somewhat better than boys.

23. This finding is consistent with what has been found previously with schoolchildren of various ages and of both genders. Here, too, the reliability of answers to "normal" questions (i.e., those that are not especially difficult) showed little differentiation, whereas the reliability of answers to questions about color and to leading questions showed great variability [W. Stern, 1904, p. 101 ff.; Oppenheim, 1906, p. 73.]

24. Incidentally, things are no different for adults on average: Before they attend to color and other aesthetic aspects of a picture, the material content is absorbed, and most adults never go beyond this point.

25. In a subsequent monograph, we will discuss the many experiments that have been conducted concerning the perception of a momentarily visible picture rather than testimony based on a previously seen picture.

26. Compare the comments on p. 10 of this monograph. See further, W. Stern.

27. However, this area remains in such a state of flux that one can never draw sharp dividing lines between different stages of development. Still, even the serious activities of the child, such as eating, dressing, and so forth, are often carried out in a way that involves the play of fantasy, and easily become completely fantastic.

28. To examine the influence of these important but fleeting factors more thoroughly, data-gathering procedures other than handwriting, such as audiorecording and film, are going to be needed.

29. Groos then also mentions the well-known tale by Goethe, "The New Paris" (in the second book of *Truth and Fiction*). Because in that imaginary epoch Goethe was already 7 years old, the example does not really fit within the limits of our treatment. But we should at least take note of how, in this particular case, several of the psychological features of falsified testimony appear with paradigmatic clarity. Goethe says how happy his comrades were when he told them stories, "And they especially loved it when I spoke in the first-person and they took great pleasure that, as one of their mates, such wonderful things could happen to me. Moreover, they were not annoyed that I could find space and time for such adventures, because they seemed to know what I was occupied with, and when I came and went. . . . So they must have instead deceived themselves, to think that I could have taken them to Boston." And after the story was told, he reported, "This fairy tale, the truth of which my mates passionately tried to convince themselves, earned great applause. Each visited the place mentioned for himself alone." When repeating the tale: "I took care not to change much of the content, and as a result of the sameness of my story, I transformed the fable into truth in the souls of my listeners."

This is a case, if not with Goethe then certainly with his audience, of a very typical example of that gray area between appearance and reality, which is so characteristic of fantasized testimonies. Goethe also spoke to the moral significance of the fabrication: "If I had not gradually been able to learn, in accordance with my nature, to work these ghosts and this hot air into an artistic portrayal, the braggartly early versions would certainly not have remained without bad consequences for me." But he continued, "Incidentally, I was disinclined toward lying and pretense and in no case was I at all irresponsible." This sentence shows how little the inclination toward storytelling has to do with those falsifications of testimony that are of interest to us.

30. Sometimes the child is already so linguistically advanced that the merely defensive nature of what is said is obvious. According to private correspondence, the 3-year-old Ellen had once bitten her little brother, and after that her father named her "the biting lass." When after some days the father repeated to her, "You're the biting lass," she stamped her foot defensively and said, "*Don't, Daddy! Don't keep saying that.*" With quite the same intentions, another child might perhaps have said simply "*no, no*" and in this way created the appearance of a denial.

31. Cf. p. 107 f. of this book.

32. "Pseudophobia" among older children, of the sort portrayed by Stanley Hall [1902, p. 119] is an example of such a sickness.

33. Translator's note: Although Clara and William Stern wrote brief introductions for Parts I and II, they did not do so for Part III.

34. Relevant entries in the bibliography at the end of the book include works by Dürr-Borst [1906], Kosog [1907], Oppenheim [1906a, 1906b], Stern [1905].

35. The special relationship between the way in which questions are asked and lying will be discussed in the next chapter.

36. In the rare cases of experimental investigation, of course, leading questions are admissible.

37. For a more thorough orientation vis-à-vis the general problem of psychogenetic causation and the theoretical concept of convergence invoked, the reader is referred to the essay W. Stern [1907].

38. Another pedagog of past times, the well-known philanthropist Chr. G. Saltzmann, made an astute observation in this regard. In his ironic *The Little Book of Crabs, or Advice on Unreasonable Child-Rearing Practices* [1807], one section is titled "How to Teach a Child to Lie," and there is a subsection under the heading "Punish Your Children When They Tell the Truth!" The scenes he relates are worth reading in the original.

39. Saltzmann characterizes such unpedagogical behavior with intentional coarseness—but nevertheless very emphatically—by the maxim, "By what you say, give children reason to lie" ([1807], pp. 121–122).

40. Saltzmann has also skillfully captured this pedagogical misstep. The following stems from a conversation between a mother and her child, who has just returned home from visiting a friend ([1807], p. 123 f.):

"So, did you see little Caroline's mother?"
"Yes, she was there."
"What was she wearing?"
"I didn't notice."
"But of coarse you must have seen. Was she wearing her print dress or the linen one?"
"I think she was wearing the printed dress."
"Well you silly girl! 'I think it was the printed one.' Don't you know?"
"Yes, now I remember. It was the printed dress."

"Didn't Caroline tell you who will be visiting them this evening?"
"No, I didn't ask her."
"Well you silly goose. . . . Didn't Caroline say anything about Mr. Paten?"
"Not as far as I know."
"He's going there this evening."
"Yes, now I remember. He's going there this evening."

41. The reference here is to Johann Paul Friedrich Richter, a German author who lived from 1763–1825. His *Levana oder Erziehungslehre (Levana, or Principles of Childrearing)* was published in 1807.

42. Translator's note: Clearly, the Sterns doubted the fidelity of some of Rousseau's notions about childrearing to the life circumstances in which children *naturally* find themselves, and in this specific instance branded Rousseau's as the opposite of natural—in other words, as artificial and unnatural.

43. For literature relevant to the general question of legal hearings, the

reader is directed to the bibliography at the end of the book, part C, and especially the works by Baginsky [1907], Behrend [1908], Michel [1907], Schmidt [1906], Schkeickert [1906], Stern [1908].

44. The following case, reported by Ledenig [1908], serves as an example. Following a domestic argument with her husband, a construction worker's wife committed suicide. At first, the man was suspected of having murdered her (by hanging her in the pantry), and he was arrested. Luckily for him, the statement of the dead woman's 3½ year-old daughter helped to gain his release. The little girl had been with the mother right up to the time of the incident in the pantry. The next day, the little girl had told her aunt about the course of events, and then told the same thing to the investigative judge (p. 255): "On Sunday morning, the mother argued with the father and struck him. He went into his room, while the mother stayed in the kitchen. . . . Mama kissed the little girl and told her she was good. Mama helped the little girl pull on her stockings, gave her a bonnet, and told her to tell father that she (mother) had gone into the pantry to get dressed. The little girl heard mother lock herself in from the inside. Father broke the door open, brought mother out, and placed her onto the bed and splashed water on her. At this point, many people came. . . . In no way did the child's report seem like a story that the child had been instructed to tell." Surely, there is much in this account that the child could not have said in just that way (for example, a child of this age cannot make a determination such as Sunday morning). Nevertheless, the testimony is quite rich in details of which the questioner could not have had enough knowledge to have asked leading questions (the mother's words, stockings, bonnet, and so forth). Therefore, the testimony gives the impression of conveying a recollection that is essentially accurate, and deserves the confidence that the judge showed in it.

# REFERENCES

Ament, W. (1899). *Die Entwicklung von Sprechen und Denken beim Kinde (The development of speech and thought in the child)*. Leipzig.

Ament, W. (n.d.). *Die Seele des Kindes (The mind of the child)*. Stuttgart: Kosmos.

Baginsky, A. (1907). Die Impressionabilität des Kindes unter dem Einfluß des Milieus (The impressionability of the child under the influence of the milieu). In K. L. Schäfer (Ed.), *Bericht über den Kongreß für Kinderforschung in Berlin* (pp. 10–27). Lagensalza.

Bäumer, G., & Droescher, A. (1908). *Von der Kinderseele (From the mind of the child)*. Beiträge zur Kindespsychologie aus Dichtung und Biographie (Contributions to child psychology from literature and biography). Leipzig.

Behrend. (1908). Die Zeugenaussagen von Kindern vor Gericht (Legal testimony by children). *Monatschrift für Kriminalpsychologie, 5*, 307–321.

Compayré, G. (1990). *Die Entwicklung der Kindesseele (The development of the child's mind; German translation by Ufer)*. Altenburg. (Original French editions 1893 and 1896)

Delbrück, A. (1891). *Die pathologische Lüge und die psychisch-abnormen Schwindler (The pathological lie and the psychologically deviant swindler)*. Stuttgart.

Deville, G. (1890–1891). Notes sur le développement du langage (Notes on the development of language). *Revue de linguistique et de philologie comparative (Review of Linguistics and Comparative Philology), 23*, 330–343; *24*, 10–42, 128–143, 242–257, 300–320.

Deutsch, W. (1991). *Die verborgene Aktualität von William Stern (The hidden currency of William Stern)*. Frankfurt am Main: Verlag Peter Lang.

Diehl, A. (1903). Zum Studium der Merkfähigkeit (Studies in perceptiveness). *Beiträge zur Psychologie der Aussage, 1*(2), 130.

Duprat, G. L. (1903). *Le mensonge (The lie)*. Paris: Alcan.

Dürr-Borst, M. (1906). Die Erziehung der Aussage und Anschauung des Schulkindes (The training of testimony and the perspective of the schoolchild). *Die experimentelle Pädagogik, 3*, 1–30.

Dyroff, A. (1904). *Über das Seelenleben des Kindes (On the psychological life of the child)*. Bonn.

Egger, E. (1903). *Beobachtungen und Betrachtungen über die Entwicklung der Intelligenz und der Sprache bein den Kindern (Observations and considerations on the development of intelligence and language among children; German translation by H. Gassner)*. Leipzig.

Feucht. (1907). Momentaufnahmen geistiger Entwicklung eines Kindes in den ersten Lebensjahren. Die Mutter (Oswalt: Moments in the psychological development of a child in the first years of life. The mother). *Zeitscrift für Verbreitung anerkannter Gesundheits-und Erziehungslehren, 5*(2), 17–27; (5), 92–101; (8), 163–170; (12) 258–268.

Friedrich, G. (1906). Psychologische Beobachtungen an 2 Knaben (Psychological observations of two boys). In Koch, Trüberm & Ufer (Eds.), *Beiträge zur Kinderforschung und Heilerziehung (Contributions to the study of children and therapeutic childrearing)*.

Groos, K. (1908). *Die Spiele des Menschen (The games people play)*. Jena.

Hall, G. S. (1902). *Selected contributions to child psychology and pedagogy*. Altenburg.

Jaffa, S. (1903). Ein psychologisches Experiment im kriminalist. Seminar (A psychological experiment in a criminality seminar). *Beiträge zur Psychologie der Aussage, 1*(1), 91.

Kosog, O. (1907). Wahreheit und Unwahrheit bei Schulkindern (Truth and untruth among schoolchildren). *Die Deutsche Schule, 11*, 65–78.

Lamiell, J. T. (1996). William Stern: More than "the IQ guy." In G. A. Kimble, C. Alan Boneau, & M. Wertheimer (Eds.), *Portrait of Pioneers in Psychology* (Vol. II, pp. 73–85). Hillsdale, NJ: Erlbaum.

Ledenig. (1908). Zur Frage der Zeugenwahrnehmung (On the question of the witness's perception). *Gross' Archiv für Kriminologische Anthropologie, 29*, 248 ff.

Lindner, G. (1898). *Aus dem Naturgarten der Kindersprache (From the natural garden of children's speech)*. Leipzig.

Lipmann, O., & Wendriner, E. (1906). Aussageesperimente im Kindergartern (Experiments in Kindergarten). *Beiträge zur Psychologie der Aussage, 2*, 418–423.

Lobsien, M. (1903). Aussage und Wirklichkeit bei Schulkindern (Testimony and reality among schoolchildren). *Beiträge zur Psychologie der Aussage, 1*(2), 130.

Lobsien, M. (1905). Über das Gedächtnis für bildlich dargestellte Dinge in siener Abhängigkeit von der Zwischenzeit (On memory for photographed objects and its dependence on time). *Beiträge zur Psychologie der Aussage, 2*(2), 17 ff.

Major, D. R. (1906). *First steps in mental growth*. New York.

Marcinowski. (1905). Zur Frage der "Lüge bei Kindern unter vier Jahren" (On the question of "lying among children under four years old"). *Zeitscrift für pädagogische Psychologie, 10*, 17–33.

Meumann, E. (1907). *Vorlesungen zur Einführung in die experimentelle Pädagogik und ihre psychologischen Grundlagen (Introductory lectures on experimental pedagogy and its psychological foundations)*. Leipzig: Verlag von Wilhelm Englemann.

Michel, O. H. (1907). Die Zeugnisfähigkeit der Kinder vor Gericht (Children's testimonial abilities in court). *Pädagogisches Magazin, 312*.

Oppenheim, R. (1906a). Der Erinnerungsunterrict. Seine Notwendigkeit und seine Form (Teaching recollection: Its necessity and its form). *Frauenbildung, 5*, 507–509.

Oppenheim, R. (1906b). Über die Erziehbarkeit der Aussage bei Schulkindern (On the educability of schoolchildren in the giving of testimony). *Beiträge zur Psychologie der Aussage, 2*(3), 52–98.

Perez, B. (1902). *Les trois premières années de l'enfant (The first three years of the child)*. 6th ed.

Piper, H. (1906). Die pathologische Lüge (The pathological lie). *Zeitschrift für pädagogische Psychologie, 8*, 1–15.

Preyer, W. (1905). *Die Seele des Kindes (The mind of the child)*. 1st ed. 1888. (Revised by K. L. Schäefer, Leipzig, 1905)

Rousseau, J.-J. (1762). Émile ou de le'éducation (Émile, or on education). Paris.

Saltzmann, C. G. (1807). *Krebsbüchlein oder Anweigsung zu einer unvernünftigen Erziehung der Kinder (Little book of crabs, or advice on unreasonable child-rearing practices)*. 4th ed. Erfurt.

Schäfer, K. L. (1905). Kommen Lügen bei Kindern vor dem vierten Jahre vor? (Do children lie before the age of four?) *Zeitschrift für pädagogische Psychologie, 7*, 195–201.

Schmidt, F. (1908). Zur Psychologie der Zeugenaussagen (On the psychology of witness testimony). *Monatschrifte für Kriminalpsychologie, 5*, 321–324.

Schneickert, H. (1906). Das Kind als Zeuge im Strafverfahren (The child as witness in criminal proceedings). *Beiträge zur Psychologie der Aussage, 2*(4), 140–145.

Scupin, E., and Scupin, G. (1907). *Bubi's erste Kindheit. Ein Tagebuch (Bubi's early childhood. A diary)*. Leipzig.

Stern, C., & Stern, W. (1907). *Die Kindersprache (Children's speech)*. Leipzig: Barth.

Stern, C., & Stern, W. (1909). *Erinnerung, Aussage und Lüge in der ersten Kindheit (Recollection, testimony, and lying in early childhood)*. Leipzig: Barth.

Stern, W. (1902). Zur Psychologie der Aussage (Experimentelle Untersuchungen über Erinnerungstreue) [On the Psychology of Testimony (Experimental Investigations on the Accuracy of Recollection)]. *Zeitschrift für die gesasmte Strafwissenschaft, 22*, 315–373.

Stern, W. (1904a). Die Aussage als geistige Leistung und als Verhörsproduct: Experimentelle Schüleruntersuchungen (Testimony as a psychological act and in response to questioning: Experimental investigations with schoolchildren). *Beiträge zur Psychologie der Aussage, 1*(3).

Stern, W. (1904b). Wirklichkeitsversuche (Studies of what really happened). *Beiträge zur Psychologie der Aussage, 1*, 1–31.

Stern, W. (1905). Kinderaussagen und Aussagepädagogik (Children's testimony and the pedagogy of testimony). *Zeitscrift für pädagogische Psychologie, 7*, 192–195.

Stern, W. (1906). *Person und Sache: System der philosophischen Weltanschauung, Band 1: Ableitung und Grundlehre (Person and thing: A systematic philosophical world view, Volume 1: Philosophical foundations)*. Leipzig: Barth.

Stern, W. (1908a). Tatsachen und Ursachen der seelischen Entwicklung (Facts and causes of psychological development). *Zeitschrift für angewandte Psychologie und psychologische Sammelforschung, 1*, 1.

Stern, W. (1908b). Zur Psychologie der Kinderaussagen (On the psychology of testimony by children). *D. Jur.-Ztg., 13*, 51–57.

Stern, W. (1914). *Psychologie der frühen Kindheit bis zum sechsten Lebenshahr*. Leipzig: Barth. [English translation: Barwell, A. (1924). *The psychology of early childhood through the sixth year of life*. (New York: Henry Holt).

Stern, W. (1918). *Person und Sache: System der philosophischen Weltanschauung, Band 2: Die menschliche Persönlichkeit* [Person and thing: A systematic philosophical world view, Volume 2: The human personality]. Leipzig: Barth.

Stern, W. (1924). *Person and Sache: System der kritischen Personalismus, Band 3: Wertphilosophie* (Person and thing: System of critical personalism, Volume 3: Philosophy of values). Leipzig: Barth.

Stern, W. (1927). Selbstdarstellung. In R. Schmidt, *Die Philosophie der Gegenwart in Selbstdarstellungen* (pp. 128–184). Leipzig: Meiner. [English translation: Langer, S. (1930). William Stern: Autobiography. In C. Murchison (Ed.), *A history of psychology in autobiography* (Vol. 1, pp. 335–388). Worcester, MA: Clark University Press.]

Stern, W. (1935). *Allgemeine Psychologie auf personalistischer Grundlage* (General psychology from a personalistic standpoint). The Haag, Netherlands: Nijhoff. [English translation: Spoerl, H. (1939). *General psychology from a personalistic standpoint.* (New York: Macmillan).]

Stern, W., & Stern, C. (1905). Erinnerung und Aussage in der ersten Kindheit: Ein Kapitel aus der Psychogenesis eines Kindes (Recollection and testimony in early childhood: A chapter from the psychological development of a child). *Beiträge zur Psychologie der Aussage, 2*(2), 31–67.

Sully, J. (1897). *Studies of childhood 1895.* Leipzig: Deutsch & Stimpfl.

Tiedemeann, D. (1787). *Beobachtungen über die Entwicklung der Seelenfähigkeiten bein Kindern* (Observations on the development of psychological capabilities among children). (New edition by Ufer. Altenburg 1897)

Wolfert. (1901). Zur Entwicklung der Sprache des Kindes (On the development of speech in children). *Die Kinderfehler, 6,* 176–181.

# BIBLIOGRAPHY

## A. Works Pertaining to Early Childhood Generally.

In this section are listed not only those works that are relevant to early childhood development in general but also those that in places touch on the theme of recollection, testimony, and lying and for this reason have been referenced in the present text.

1. W. Ament. *Die Entwicklung von Sprechen und Denken beim Kinde.* (*The development of speech and thought in the child.*) Leipzig: 1899. 233 S.
2. ———*Die Seele des Kindes.* (*The mind of the child.*) Stuttgart, Kosmos. (Ohne Jahr.) 96 S.
3a. G. Bäumer and A. Droescher. *Von der Kinderseele.* Beiträge zur Kindespsychologie aus Dichtung und Biographie. (*From the mind of the child.* Contributions to child psychology from literature and biography.) Leipzig: 1908.
3. G. Compayré. *Die Entwicklung der Kindesseele.* Deutsch von Ufer. (*The development of the child's mind.* German (translation) by Ufer.) Altenburg: 1900. (Französische Originalausgaben 1893 und 1896). Insbesondere S. 387–390.
4. G. Deville. *Notes sur le dévoloppement du langage.* (*Observations on the development of language.*) Rev. de linguistique et de philol compar. 23, 330–343. 24, 10–42, 128–143, 242–257, 300–320. 1890–1891.
5. A. Dyroff. *Über das Seelenleben des Kindes.* (*On the psychological life of the child.*) Bonn: 1904. 59 S.
6. E. Egger. *Beobachtungen und Betrachtungen über die Entwicklung der Intelligenz und der Sprache bei den Kindern.* Deutsch von H. Gassner. (*Observations and considerations on the development of intelligence and language among children.* German (translation) by H. Gassner.) Leipzig: 1903. 73 S.
7. Prof. Feucht. *Oswalt: Momentaufnahmen geistiger Entwicklung eines Kindes in den ersten Lebensjahren.* Die Mutter. (*Oswalt: Moments in the psychological development of a child in the first years of life.* The mother.) Zeitschrift für Verbreitung anerk. Gesundheits-u. Erziehungslehren, 5(2), S. 17–27; (5), S. 92–101; (8), S. 163–170; (12), S. 258–268. 1907.
8. G. Friedrich. *Psychologische Beobachtungen an 2 Knaben.* Beiträge zur Kinderforschung und Heilerziehung. (*Psychological observations of two boys.* Contributions to the study of children and therapeutic childrearing.) Herausgegeben von Koch, Trüper, Ufer. Heft XVII. 1906.
9. R. Gaupp. *Psychologie des Kindes.* Aus Natur und Geisteswelt. (*Psychology of the child.* From Nature and the World of the Mind.) 213. Leipzig, 1908. 154 S. Insbesondere S. 64–67.
10. K. Groos. *Das Seelenleben des Kindes.* (*The psychological life of the child.*) 2. Auflage. Berlin: 1908. 260 S.
11. ———*Die Spiele des Menschen* (*Games people play.*) Jena: 1899.

---

Translator's note: Bibliography appears as it does in original, with only the addition of English translations in parentheses.

12. G. Lindner. *Aus dem Naturgarten der Kindersprache.* (*From the natural garden of children's speech.*) Leipzig: 1898. 122 S.
13. D. R. Major. *First steps in mental growth.* New York: 1906. 360 pages.
14. B. Perez. *Les trois premières années de l'enfant.* (*The child's first three years.*) 6. Auflage. 1902.
15. W. Preyer. *Die Seele des Kindes.* (*The mind of the child.*) Erste Auflage 1888. Sechste Auflage, bearbeitet von K. L. Schäfer, Leipzig, 1905 (nach dieser im Text zitiert).
16. J. J. Rousseau. *Émile ou de l'éducation.* (*Emile or an education.*)
17. E. and G. Scupin. *Bubi's erste Kindheit. Ein Tagebuch.* (*Bubi's early childhood. A diary.*) Leipzig: 1907. 263 S.
18. J. Sully. *Studies of childhood 1895.* Übersetzung: *Untersuchungen über die Kindheit.* Deutsch v. Stimpfl. Leipzig: 1897. Insbesondere S. 235–248.
19. D. Tiedemann. *Beobachtungen über die Entwicklung der Seelenfähigkeiten bei Kindern.* (*Observations on the development of psychological capabilities among children.*) 1787. Neu herausgegeben von Ufer. Altenburg 1897. 56 S.
20. Wolfert. *Zur Entwicklung der Sprache des Kindes. Die Kinderfehler.* (*On the development of speech in children. Children's mistakes.*) 6, S. 176–181. 1901.

B. On Children's Lies

The following list contains works relating not only to early childhood but also to schoolaged children.

21. *Beiträge zur Psychologie und Pädagogik der Kinderlügen und Kinderaussagen.* (*Contributions to the psychology and pedagogy of children's lies and testimony.*) (Veröffentlichungen des Vereins für Kindespsychologie zu Berlin.) Bisher 13 Nummern. *Zeitschrift für pädagogische Psychologie* (Kemsies-Hirschlaff), 7, S. 177–205; 8, S. 81–124, 1906; 10, S. 17–33, 1908.—Vergleich im einzelnen: Kemsies, Lipmann, Lowinsky, Marcinowski, Poppelreuter, Schäfer, Stern, Viemann.
22. J. Delitsch. *Über Kinderlügen.* (*On children's lies.*) *Pädagogische psychologische Studien* (Brahn) 4, S. 24; 29–32. 1903.
23. A. Delbrück. *Die pathologische Lüge und die psychisch-abnormen Schwindler.* (*The pathological lie and the psychologically deviant swindler.*) Stuttgart: 1891.
24. G. L. Duprat. *Le mensonge.* (*The lie.*) Paris, Alcan. 1903. 188 S.
25. F. Kemsies. *Einführung* (zu den Beiträge zur Psychologie der Kinderlügen und Kinderaussagen). [*Introduction* (to the contributions to the psychology of children's lies and children's testimony)]. *Zeitscrift für pädagogische Psychologie* (Kemsies Hirschlaff), 7, S. 177–182. 1905. Mit Literaturübersicht.
26. ———*Zur Einteilung der Lügen und Aussagen.* (*Classifying lies and testimony.*) Ebda. S. 183–192. 1905.
27. Fr. Lembke. *Die Lüge, unter besonderer Berücksichtigung der Volksschulerziehung.* (*The lie, with special reference to public school education.*) *Deutscher Blätter für erzieherische Unterricht.* 1901, Nr. 21–26 und; *Pädagogisches Magazin* (Mann). Heft 171.
28. Otto Lipmann. *Einige interessante Kinderlügen.* (*Some interesting lies told by children.*) *Zeitschrift für pädagogische Psychologie,* 8, S. 85–88. 1906.

29. V. Lowinski. G. L. Duprat, *Die Lüge*. (*The lie.*) *Zeitschrift für pädagogische Psychologie*, 10, S. 17–33. 1908.

30. Marcinowski. *Zur Frage der "Lüge bei Kindern unter vier Jahren."* (*On the question of "lying by children under four years old."*) *Zeitschrift für pädagogische Psychologie*, 7, S. 201–205. 1905.

31. N. N. *Eine Statistik über Schulunredlichkeit*. (*A statistic on dishonesty in the schools.*) *Neue Jahrbuch für d. klass. Altert. etc. und für Pädagogik*. (Ilberg-Gerth), 21–22, S. 307–312. 1908.

32. Gertrud Pappenheim. *Über das Lügen der Kinder*. (*On the lies of children.*) *Kindergarten*, 34, S. 137–152, 165–179. 1903.

33. H. Piper. *Die pathologische Lüge*. (*The pathological lie.*) *Zeitschrift für pädagogische Psychologie*, 8, S. 1–15. 1906.

34. Chr. G. Saltzmann. *Krebsbüchlein oder Anweisung zu einer unvernünftigen Erziehung der Kinder*. (*Little book of crabs, or advice on unreasonable childrearing practices.*) Vierte Auflage. Erfurt: 1807.

35. K. L. Schäfer. *Kommen Lügen bei Kindern vor dem vierten Jahre vor?* (*Do children lie before the age of four?*) *Zeitschrift für pädagogische Psychologie*, 7, S. 195–201. 1905.

36. A. Schinz. *La moralité l'enfant*. (*The morality of the child.*) *Revue Philosophie*, 45, S. 259–295. 1898. Deutsch: *Die Sittlichkeit des Kindes*. von Chr. Ufer. *Beiträge zur Kinderforschung*. Heft 1. 1898.

37. G. Stanley Hall. *Selected contributions to child psychology and pedagogy*. Deutsch von Stimpfl. Altenburg 1902. Kap. IV: Das Lügen der Kinder (Children's lies.)

38. J. Trüper. *Lüge (Irrtum, Unwahrheit, Lüge)*. [*The lie (error, untruth, lie)*]. *Encyklopädische Handbuch der Pädagogik*, hrsg. von Rein. 2. Auflage, 1906. 18 S. (Mit reichhaltigem Literaturverzeichnis.)

39. W. Viemann. *Beispiele von Kinderlügen bei großen Männern* (*Examples of children's lies among big men.*) *Zeitschrift für pädagogische Psychologie*, 8, S. 81–84. 1906.


C. Testimony, Capability of the Child As a Witness in Legal Proceedings,
and Educating Children in Giving Testimony
(also contains literature pertaining to schoolaged children)


40. A. Baginsky. *Die Impressionabilität des Kindes unter dem Einfluß des Milieus*. (*The impressionability of the child under the influence of the milieu.*) Bericht über den Kongreß für Kinderforschung in Berlin (K. L. Schäfer). Langensalza 1907. S. 10–27.

41. *Beobachtungen über nichtpathologische Erinnerungstäuschungen bei Schulkindern*. (*Observations on non-pathological mistakes of recollection among school children.*) *Beiträge zur Psycyologie der Aussage* (Stern), 1(1), S. 121–124. 1903.

42. Behrend. *Die Zeugenaussagen von Kindern von Kindern vor Gericht*. (*Witness testimony given by children in court.*) *Monnatschrift für Kriminalpsychologie* (Aschaffenburg), 5, S. 307–321. 1908.

43. A. Binet. *La suggestibilité*. (*Suggestibility.*) Paris: 1900.

44. Marie Borst. *Experimentelle Untersuchungen über die Erziehbarkeit und die Treue*

*der Aussage.* (*Experimental investigations of the educability and validity of testimony.*) Beiträge zur Psychologie der Aussage (Stern), 2(1), S. 73–120. 1905.

45. Marie Dürr-Borst. *Die Erziehung der Aussage und Anschauung des Schulkindes.* (*The training of testimony and the perspective of the school-child.*) Die experimentelle Pädagogik (Lay-Meumann), 3, S. 1–30. 1906.

46. J. Cohn und W. Gent. *Aussage und Aufmerksamkeit.* (*Testimony and attentiveness.*) Zeitschrift für angewandte Psychologie, 1, 129–152 und 233–265.

47. A. Franken. *Eine experimentelle Untersuchung über das Wahrheitsbewußtsein bei Schulkindern.* (*An experimental investigation of the consciousness of truth among school children.*) Zeitschrift für angewandte Psychologie (Stern-Lipmann), 1, S. 266–273. 1907/8.

48. L. F. Göbelbecker. *Harmloses kindliches Gedankenspiel oder phantastische Lüge, abnorme Selbsttäuschung oder pathologische Einbildung?* (*Harmless childish mind games or fantastic lies, abnormal self-deception or pathological imagination?*) Experimentelle Pädagogik (Meumann), 5, S. 50–63. 1907.

49. H. Gross. *Kriminalpsychologie.* (*Criminal psychology.*) Second edition. Leipzig: 1905. Insbesondere S. 474–486.

50. P. Hösel. *Aussagepsychologie und Schule.* (*The psychology of testimony and the school.*) Deutsche Schulpraxis, 25, Nr. 9, 10, und 11.

51. O. Kosog. *Suggestion einfacher Sinneswahrnehmungen bei Schulkindern.* (*The suggestion of simple sensory perceptions among school children.*) Beiträge zur Psychologie der Aussage (Stern), 2(3), S. 99–114. (1906).

52. ——*Wahrheit und Unwahrheit bei Schulkindern.* (*Truth and untruth among school children.*) Die deutsche Schule, 11, S. 65–78. 1907.

53. Ledenig. *Zur Frage der Zeugenwahrnehmung.* (*On the question of the witness's perception.*) Gross' Archiv für Krim. Anthrop. 29, S. 248f. 1908.

54. Otto Lipmann. *Die Wirkung von Suggestivfragen.* (*The effect of suggestive questions.*) Zeitschrift für angewandte Psychologie (Stern-Lipmann), 1, S. 44–92, 382–415, 504–546; 2, S. 198–242. 1907/8. Auch separat: Leipzig. 1908.

55. O. Lipmann und E. Wendriner. *Aussageexperimente im Kindergarten.* (*Experiments on testimony in kindergarten.*) Beiträge zur Psychologie der Aussage (Stern), 2, S. 418–423. 1906.

56. ——*Reformvorschläge zur Zeugenwahrnehmung von Standpunkte des Psychologen.* (*Suggested reforms concerning witnesses' perceptions from the standpoint of a psychologist.*) Gross' Archiv für Krim.-Anthro., 20, S. 68–81.

57. Marx Lobsien. *Aussage und Wirklichkeit bei Schulkindern.* (*Testimony and reality among school children.*) Beiträge zur Psychologie der Aussage (Stern), 1(2), S. 26–89.

58. O. H. Michel. *Die Zeugnisfähigkeit der Kinder vor Gericht.* (*Children's testimonial abilities in court.*) Pädagogisches Magazin (Mann). 312. Heft. Langensalza 1907. 67 S.

59. Motet. *Les faux témoignages des enfants devant la justice.* (*The false testimony of the child in court.*) Annales d'hygiène publique et de médecine légale. Série 3. Bd. 17, No. 6. 1887.

60. Rosa Oppenheim. *Über die Erziehbarkeit der Aussage bei Schulkindern.* (*On the educability of school children in the giving of testimony.*) Beiträge zur Psychologie der Aussage (Stern), 2(3), S. 52–98. 1906.

61. ———*Der Erinnerungsunterricht. Seine Notwendigkeit und seine Form. (Teaching recollection: Its necessity and its form.)* Frauenbildung, 5, S. 507–509.

62. W. Poppelreuter. *Zur Psychologie des Wahrheitsbewußtseins. (On the psychology of consciousness of truth.)* Zeitschrift für pädagogische Psychologie, 8, S. 104–117. 1906.

63. F. Schmidt. *Zur Psychologie der Zeugenaussagen. (On the psychology of witness testimony.)* Monnatschrifte für Kriminalpsychologie (Aschaffenburg), 5, S. 321–324. 1908.

64. H. Schneickert. *Das Kind als Zeuge im Strafverfahren. (The child as witness in criminal proceedings.)* Beiträge zur Psychologie der Aussage (Stern), 2(4), S. 140–145.

65. W. Stern. *Die Aussage als geistige Leistung und als Verhörsprodukt. Experimentelle Schüleruntersuchungen. (Testimony as a psychological act and in response to questioning:* Experimental investigations with school children.) *Beiträge zur Psychologie der Aussage (Stern), 1(3);* auch separat: Leipzig, 1904. 147 S.

66. ———*Zur Psychologie der Kinderaussagen. (On the psychology of testimony by children.)* D. Jur.-Ztg., 13, S. 51–57.

67. ———*Kinderaussagen und Aussagepädagogik. (Children's testimony and the pedgogy of testimony.)* Zeitschrift für pädagogische Psychologie (Kemsies-Hirschlaff), 7, S. 192–195.

68. ———*Leitzätze über die Bedeutung der Aussagepsychologie für das gerichtliche Verfahren. (Tenets pertaining to the significance of psychological astudies of testimony for legal proceedings.)* Beiträge zur Psychologie der Aussage (Stern), 2(2), S. 73–80. 1906.

# INDEX